Essential
Rome

by

CAROLE CHESTER

Carole Chester has written 30 travel books
and contributes regularly to
several publications.
She trained in journalism on Fleet Street
and is a frequent visitor to Rome.

Produced by the Publishing Division of
The Automobile Association

Written by Carole Chester
Peace and Quiet Section
by Paul Sterry
Consultant: Frank Dawes

Edited, designed and produced by
the Publishing Division of The
Automobile Association. Maps ©
The Automobile Association 1991.

Distributed in the United Kingdom
by the Publishing Division of The
Automobile Association, Fanum
House, Basingstoke, Hampshire,
RG21 2EA.

A CIP catalogue record for this
book is available from the British
Library.

ISBN 07495 0083-2

Published by The Automobile
Association.

Typesetting: Avonset, Midsomer
Norton, Bath.
Colour separation: Mullis Morgan
Ltd, London.
Printing: Printers S.R.L., Trento,
Italy.
Front cover picture: Colosseum

This book employs a simple rating system to help choose which places to visit:

◆◆◆　do not miss

◆◆　　see if you can

◆　　　worth seeing if you have time

INTRODUCTION

It is noisy, frenetic and traffic-jammed but as 'eternal' as its clichéd nickname suggests. For Rome, city of the Caesars, has survived as Italy's administrative and cultural capital and the seat of power of the Roman Catholic faith. Despite the physical threats to its foundations from war, pollution and the motor car, its ancient monuments have withstood the test of time, attracting tourists from around the globe in their millions, whatever the time of year, whatever the kind of weather. They come not only to admire the monumental arches and the masterpieces of art, but to experience *la dolce vita* in a city which gave us its language, its laws and its calendar. Life

A panoramic view across the 'Eternal City'

is not always so sweet here, of course, with the hazards of bag snatchers and erratic drivers or the frustrations of Roman bureaucracy. But it is sweet enough to shrug off the unlikely possibility of being kidnapped (the local populace is more volatile than violent) or falling into the poisonous waters of the River Tevere, or as we know it, the Tiber. It is sweet enough to risk the effects of exhaust fumes and the fluctuations of the lira in return for a first-hand look at aeons of treasures and gastronomic indulgences. Tourists, like the residents, put up with the chaos and cacophony because, well, you know . . . when in Rome . . .

Rome grew from a simple farming community scattered over seven hills east of the Tiber into a walled city in the 4th century BC. Expansion over subsequent centuries required the building of the Aurelian Wall in the 3rd century AD, taking in a much larger area including that district across the Tiber now known as Trastevere. That second wall still defines the city centre, although building and population has spread well beyond it, and there are now over three million

The stunning symmetry of St Peter's Square seen from the dome of the basilica

inhabitants. Once you are in the city, you will realise that, to adopt another old adage, 'you can't see Rome in a day'. There is so much to see and take in that, apart from a general tour to get your bearings, you must be selective. Even those with special interests such as art or architecture must make their priority choices, and what you wish to see the most may point to where you stay. But you will find history even without seeking it – with a statue or fountain round every corner. Modern Romans are so used to it all they hurry by on their way to the office or café without stopping at all. Of the celebrated hills, though, you will see little, as, except for the Aventine Hill, they are no longer prominent. Suburban areas such as Parioli have become fashionable and boast more exclusive hotels and nightclubs than the Via Vittorio Veneto. Yet the city's main squares, notably Piazza di Spagna, are still the most popular rendezvous points; the hubs of activity.

Rome is ancient but always vital. The days of its glorious Empire are dead but city life is very much alive. Whether or not you follow the custom of tossing a coin into the Trevi Fountain you will want to come back – again and again.

BACKGROUND

According to legend, Rome was founded by Romulus (the first of seven kings of Rome) together with his brother, Remus, in 753 BC. According to fact, the seven hills of Rome were a scattered farming community until 600 BC. The area was part of a kingdom ruled first by the Sabine kings, then by the Etruscans, who laid the very first foundations of what was to become a monumental city. Marshy land (later to become the Forum) was drained, a sewage system started and a temple planned for Capitoline Hill. In 509 BC Tarquinius 'The Proud' was driven out and what had been a kingdom became a republic, which, despite invasions and wars, grew steadily more powerful. The Punic Wars, between 264 and 241 BC and 214 and 201 BC, in spite of Hannibal's celebrated crossing of the Alps, resulted in the defeat of Carthage. At the end of the third Punic War, Rome successfully crushed and destroyed Carthage altogether.

The Roman Empire

Although the first Roman general to use his troops for political moves was the dictator, Sulla (81 to 79 BC), the most famous leader to follow this pattern was Julius Caesar, who mastered Gaul, Britain and Italy and transformed the Roman Republic into an Empire. After Caesar's assassination in the Senate, it was his great nephew, Octavian, who became the first Roman emperor. We know him better as Augustus, and it was in his reign that an extensive building programme was initiated. This was also an age when culture blossomed – the age of Ovid and Virgil. Even today there are remnants of the time of Augustus: the ruins of the Roman theatre dedicated to his nephew, Marcellus; the altar of Augustan Peace erected by order of the Senate to celebrate the peace established by Augustus over all Roman-occupied territories; his mausoleum and the House of Livia, said to be the house where Augustus and his empress lived on Palatine Hill.

Ruins from the Roman Empire on Palatine Hill

The Capitoline Wolf – an Etruscan bronze with Romulus and Remus added during the Renaissance

Life Before Christ

Until the early part of the 6th century, Romans had no temples – merely turf altars in the open. Legend tells that those early shepherd soldiers brought any spoils of war to a sacred oak tree that grew on the Capitol. What is fact is that the kings built the first great temple here, though the Republic was born before it was consecrated in 509 BC. Dedicated to Jupiter, Juno and Minerva, it was more simply known as the Temple of Jupiter and was the centre of Rome's religious life. It was here that the Senate held its first session each year and celebrated Roman victories.

The early Romans were deeply religious, recognising an air of mystery in everything about them, which is why Jupiter came to represent the sky, and Mars (later to become the god of war) first represented the fields. Religion was part of daily life so that houses, gates and stores were all presided over by deities. There was also a good community spirit and the earliest identifiable sites in the Forum were of both a religious and social nature. Though the Forum was eventually enlarged to embrace the whole valley, its heart was the very first meeting place (*Comitium*) – a small square before the official Senate rendezvous (*Curia*) and the larger open space or Forum proper beside the Via Sacra. It was the hub of city life, the scene of religious and triumphant ceremonies, sacrifices and important funerals and also a law court where the *praetor*, seated on his tribunal, gave judgment in front of the populace. After the demise of the Republic, the Palatine, not the Forum, became the real centre of the Roman world.

Life After Christ

From AD 54 to 68 Nero was emperor, a man of orgiastic appetites. He was noted for frivolous spending, having Pompeii's Roman Theatre gilded inside and out in a day just for the reception of King Tiridates of Armenia in AD 66 and it was he who 'fiddled while Rome burned' during the great fire of AD 64. He blamed the fire on the Christians and initiated their persecution. His fantastic palace, the Domus Aurea (Golden House) on the Esquiline Hill, some of which may be seen today, was entirely gilded and was furnished in the utmost luxury. Over the next three reigns the Colosseum was built. Vespasian had the idea, thinking of it as a way of returning to the people some of the land Nero had taken, but it was not yet finished when he died in AD 79. It was inaugurated by his son Titus in AD 80 but only finally completed during Domitian's reign, AD 81–96. The 1st century AD was an era of debauchery when, as satirist Juvenal pointed out, the populace had sold its power 'for bread and circuses'. He was referring to the free food doled out once a month to thousands at the Portico Minicius and free entertainment (the slaughtering of lions, elephants and Christians and gladiatorial fights) given on such a scale that for each working day of the year, Romans enjoyed a holiday. Not all Romans approved, and many converted to Christianity, but anti-Christian activities included the destruction of the Temple at Jerusalem during the reign of Titus and the erection of the Arch of Titus in the Forum to celebrate the deed.

Whatever the scene in Rome, the empire continued to grow. Military campaigns during Trajan's reign (AD 98–117), extended frontiers beyond the Danube and by the end of his rule Roman territory stretched from Spain to the Caspian Sea and from Britain to North Africa. His successor, Hadrian, spent a great deal of time travelling through that Empire spreading Roman civilization. He particularly loved Greece, which influenced the design of his villa at Tivoli and Rome's best preserved ancient monument, the Pantheon.

In AD 286 Emperor Diocletian divided the empire, taking the eastern part himself and leaving Maximian to rule the west. The ruins of Diocletian's Baths are now the impressive setting for the fascinating Museo delle Terme. The empire was drawn together again by the first Christian emperor, Constantine the Great, under whose rule many basilicas and churches were built. He legalised Christianity in AD 313 and moved his capital to Byzantium, which he renamed Constantinople. The final decline and collapse of the western empire came about between AD 337 and 476. When Theodosius died in AD 395, the empire was again divided, never to be joined again. These were chaotic

BACKGROUND

years of fighting and unrest; Rome was sacked by the Goths in 410; brought into the eastern empire by the Ostrogoths, and threatened by the Lombards in 593. When Pope Stephen III appealed to the Franks for assistance against the Lombards, King Pepin the Short came to his aid, defeated the Lombards and gave part of central Italy to the pope. Pepin's son, Charlemagne, defeated the Lombards again in 774, winning complete control of Italy for the Franks and securing the power of the popes. He was crowned Holy Roman Emperor in 800. During the 9th century Rome was torn by struggles between rival princes as powerful families vied for the papacy. By the time the Saxon king Otto I became Holy Roman Emperor the popes had claimed the right to crown emperors and the emperors had claimed the right to confirm the election of popes. But in the Middle Ages under Pope Innocent III, the papacy gained the upper hand against the emperors. It was Innocent who approved the orders of St Francis and St Dominic, who first met during his reign.

Rome and the Papacy

Strife between papal and imperial parties was at its strongest in the 13th century, but when the papacy was transferred to Avignon in 1308 Rome lost its focal importance. Popular rebellion made Cola di Rienzo Rome's leader in 1347. He set out to establish a democratic republic, but was murdered in 1354. One of the few medieval houses in Rome to survive is Casa di Crescenzi, thought to be the home of Rienzo. It was built by Nicolò, son of Crescenzio and Theodora, who wished to renew the old magnificence of Rome, and added classical fragments to the walls of his house.

After the great schism, when the Church was split between rival claimants to the papacy in Avignon and Rome, Pope Martin V began to revive Rome's cultural life from 1447, and after this much of the city was reconstructed.

We can thank Pope Sixtus IV for the founding of the Capitoline collection in 1471, for some good town planning and the Ponte Sisto, from which there are some of the finest views in Rome, and which bears an inscription wishing for good health for Sixtus himself and for all who crossed the bridge. It was also to Sixtus IV's orders that the Sistine Chapel (now one of the Vatican's museums) was built and beautifully decorated by the best of Tuscan and Umbrian artists.

Another familiar name is that of Borgia. Rodrigo Borgia, later Pope Alexander VI (1492–1503), secured the papacy by bribery and indulged in flagrant nepotism, making his son Cesare a cardinal. Rodrigo's other children, by his beautiful mistress, Vanozza, were Lucrezia and the Duke of Gandia, the latter undoubtedly murdered by Cesare. The Borgia Apartment today is part of the Vatican Palace.

Pope Sixtus V (1585–90) may be considered the father of modern town planning. Unlike his predecessors, who merely wished to improve the viability of the old city, Sixtus V wanted to extend the city over the higher ground enclosed by the Aurelian wall in order to bring people back to the ancient residential areas which had been deserted since the Gothic wars. The basis for his development was a good water supply and road system, so he rebuilt Alexander Severus's aqueduct and planned a road network that radiated from S Maria Maggiore to connect it with other basilicas and places of interest.

Under Urban VIII came a great baroque period, when the pope chose Bernini (sculptor, painter and architect) to execute many of the fine 17th-century monuments existing today. Rome's prestige declined in the 18th century, at the end of which the French attacked and occupied the city and Napoleon took Pius VII into captivity (1809), annexing the papal states, which were restored to the Vatican five years later. Garibaldi and Mazzini's 1848 revolution was to lead to a unified Italy but their establishment of a republic of Rome was short-lived. Victor Emmanuel II of Sardinia and Savoy unified Italy (except for Rome) in 1861. Rome was added to the

Pope John Paul II often addresses his audience in several languages

kingdom in 1870 and became capital, confining the political powers of the popes to the Vatican.

Mussolini's march on Rome in 1922 heralded the beginning of the Fascist government in Italy, which was brought to an end after World War II, and Italy became a Republic in 1946. Since then, more sensitive popes have brought a new spirit into the Catholic church, most notably John XXIII in the 1950s and the current pope, John Paul II, the first non-Italian pope since 1523.

Architecture and Art

Some of the finest surviving early Roman monuments are in the form of columns and arches. Trajan's Column, for example, has scarcely changed from the time it was built in AD 113 and its reliefs have provided us with a mine of information about Roman and barbaric arms and warfare.

BACKGROUND

The Colosseum – Rome's greatest monument

The Column of Marcus Aurelius is another monument to military achievement which owes its survival, like Trajan's Column, to ecclesiastical ownership in the Middle Ages. The sheer scale of early Roman buildings is awesome. The Theatre of Marcellus, though changed out of all recognition since Caesar built it, and the Colosseum, are feats of engineering. The latter, a vast mass of stone, was originally raised on marshy ground. It was designed so that 50,000 often unruly people could enter, find their seats and leave with ease. Admiration for its architecture has inspired many later structures.

The city's most outstanding classical building is the Pantheon, built in the reign of Hadrian. For the most part Grecian in style, the huge circular domed hall is innovatively Roman. In ancient times, the Pantheon was covered with sheets of gilded bronze, though these were plundered by Byzantine emperor Constans II in 655 and replaced with lead by Gregory

Palazzo Venezia and Palazzo della Cancelleria, both early Renaissance buildings. In Paul II's reign the former became the first great Renaissance palace of Rome, though its beginnings, as a cardinal's residence, were modest. The latter is thought to have been built for Sixtus IV's nephew, Raffaele Riario, in the 15th century with money won from gambling.

This was also the golden age of the villa, and there is none finer than Villa Giulia, the ornate fanciful residence built for Julius II by Vignola, Ammannati and Vasari.

The Artists

So numerous were the great builders of Rome, right up to the 19th century when architecture was less memorable, that it is impossible to mention them all in this brief space. The same is true of painting and sculpture, for Rome is a treasure-house of art. The best place to get an idea of the quantities of marble statues which once stood in Rome is to visit the Vatican Museums and the Museo delle Terme in the Baths of Diocletian. You will see, too, examples of ancient Roman decorative painting and mosaic work in Nero's Golden House and the House of Livia. Countless frescos still enthral us – like Fra Angelico's work in the Chapel of Nicholas V and those by Botticelli, Ghirlandaio and Perugino in the Sistine Chapel. Michelangelo and Raphael left some of the most impressive

III in the 8th century. It survived because it was given to Boniface IV in 608 and consecrated as a Christian church.

Basilicas are another Roman contribution to architecture, though the very early ones have long since disappeared. For an impression of how the interior of an ancient basilica looked, St Paul's-without-the-Walls (S Paolo fuori le Mura) is the best example, even though it had to be reconstructed after a fire in 1823.

Palazzi (palaces) always make one think of Italy and two of Rome's most distinguished are

BACKGROUND

The Fontana del Nettuno in the beautiful baroque Piazza Navona

marks. The former's work spans more than half a century, with celebrated pieces like the Pietà, the Sistine ceiling and the Last Judgment. The latter is best known for his frescos in the papal apartments known as the Stanze.

Less familiar, but talented nevertheless, were painters like Giulio Romano, Perin del Vaga, Parmigianino and Rosso Fiorentino, who worked in Rome before its sacking in 1527 and pioneered a new style of art. Later, Pellegrino Tibaldi and Francesco Salviati became style leaders; but by the end of the 16th century local artisans were lacking inspiration. A new movement in art brought Caravaggio to the fore. He had come to Rome as a teenager in 1589 and, though his genius for realistic detail was recognised by several patrons, his life was difficult, with his name often appearing in police records. But his paintings, now to be seen in the Borghese Gallery, S Luigi dei Francesi and S Maria del Popolo, more than make up for that.

During the next generation it was Gian Lorenzo Bernini who brought the baroque style to a grand climax. One of the most talented artists of the 17th century, Bernini was the famous son of Pietro Bernini, himself a great artist. Bernini gave Rome many of its fountains and statues, and changed the appearance of many squares. You can see some of his statues in the Borghese Gallery and one of his most dramatic pieces in the Cornaso Chapel of Santa Maria della Vittoria. Some say that his arch rival, Borromini, was even more talented, though he was a difficult man. Borromini was 15 when he started his working life as a stonemason, but it was not until he was 30 that his grand chance came, in the form of a commission to design the church and monastery of San Carlo alle Quattro Fontane.

The baroque period was also noted for illusionary ceiling paintings. Among the most superb works of fantasy is the ceiling of the Barberini Palace executed by Pietro da Cortona: an allegorical painting representing Divine Providence receiving a starry crown from the figure of Immortality.

AREAS OF THE CITY

Medieval Quarter

Centred on Piazza Navona and the Pantheon, this area is known as Campus Martius or Campo Marzio from the days when it was an open plain – the 'field of Mars'. It doesn't look that way now, of course. A warren of narrow streets and alleys could hardly pass for the open space once used for military and gymnastic exercise, and only the Via and Piazza di Campo Marzio at its heart remind us of the original purpose.

In imperial times, this quarter was one of the city's greatest monumental centres: a public park and gardens where baths, theatres and arenas stood; the open place for chariot racing. Its appearance began to change in the 6th century, when the aqueducts were cut by the besieging Goths and the populace drifted from those waterless higher areas to huddle around the Campus' great monuments closer to the Tiber. Thus it became Rome's centre for many centuries to come. A medieval city grew up amid the ruins of the Campus to become filled with fine palaces and churches, all best explored on foot.

Monte Mario

This is a more recently developed, prestigious residential district on the city's outskirts. It was here that Clement VII built the Villa Madama, designed initially by Raphael. Today it is a place to get away from the fumes of central Rome's traffic and for fine views over the city.

Parioli

A wealthy and select residential district, boasting some of the city's most luxurious clubs and hotels, Parioli is enclosed by the Villa Borghese, Rome's major public park, and by the Villas Ada and Gloria.

Piazza della Repubblica

A central but less fashionable area, within close proximity of the main railway station and several major museums including the Baths of Diocletian. Many Romans still

Faded elegance in the residential Parioli district

Rome's most popular meeting place – the Spanish Steps

insist on calling this large circular area Piazza dell'Esedra, its former name. A good place to find reasonably priced accommodation.

Piazza di Spagna

This popular, central tourist area is usually filled with foreigners. It dates from the town planning time of Sixtus V, who promised that by 1590 the area would be inhabited. So it was: first by artists, and then by the hotel trade, which moved from the Campo dei Fiori quarter. The name stems from the 17th century, when the Spanish Embassy stood here. It has always attracted tourists, from Rubens to Tennyson, from Liszt to Byron and Keats, who stayed in a house overlooking the Spanish Steps.

In the 18th century, this square was called 'the English ghetto', and Via delle Carrozze (off the piazza) drew its name from the number of carriages which headed there for cleaning and repairs. Today, the district is one of the first stops for all visitors to Rome, and the heart of one of the city's smartest and priciest shopping precincts, plus some of the most venerable cafés.

Prati

A quiet middle class suburb with *pensione* (small hotels/guesthouses) galore and less expensive shopping possibilities.

Renaissance Quarter

This is the part of the old city south of Corso Vittorio Emmanuele. Much of its Renaissance atmosphere stems from the magnificent Palazzo Farnese. It is the district where you will find Campo dei Fiori, site of the market, held every day except Sunday. Before 1600 this was the centre of a smart, select residential district; after 1600, the square was used for executions. In this district lived Rodrigo Borgia, later Pope Alexander VI (1492–1503), and his mistress Vanozza Cattanei, and here, too, Benvenuto Cellini brawled and created his masterpieces, and Imperia, one of the most famous Renaissance courtesans, poisoned herself.

Palaces were built here, gambling parties were held and impressive processions passed through on their way to the Vatican.

One of the most handsome streets in this quarter is Via Giulia, a sort of elegant backwater these days, with scattered art galleries, antique shops and chic hotels. The street was named after Pope Julius II and was part of a Bramante plan as a new approach to St Peter's. In the 16th century it was the most fashionable street in Rome.

Trastevere

The poorest part of Rome in the 19th century is still a little seedy in parts. Equally, it is one of the most charming areas – especially for restaurants and evening entertainments. Trastevere inhabitants claim they are descended from ancient classical stock, but this is not really true. In imperial times, it was more a foreign colony. Sailors from Ravenna established themselves here in the 1st century and, later, the district was home to a mixed bunch of orientals and Jews. Because of its location across the Tiber, it was a separate and distinct quarter until the 14th century. It is, however, a stronghold of Roman dialect poetry and holds its own July *Noiantri* ('We Others') street festival.

Pons Cestius, built in 46BC, links the Tiberine Island with Trastevere

CENTRAL ROME

WHAT TO SEE

For the first-time visitor, an organised sightseeing tour of the city is recommended. It will give you your bearings and give you some ideas about what you would like to see or find out more about on subsequent excursions. Because history is such a key to Rome you might feel that you need a detailed guide in order to appreciate fully the majesty of its monuments and masterpieces. You must also try to be selective – make a list of your priority sights, landmarks and museums and stick to it. Use the simple rating system to help you. If you are sightseeing without the help of a guide, remember that there is an entrance fee for most places of interest and that Monday is the most usual closing day.

◆
ACCADEMIA DI S LUCA
77 Piazza Accademia di S Luca
Towards the end of the 15th century a fraternity of artists attached to a small church dedicated to St Luke (patron saint of painters) was founded, and today its home is the Palazzo Carpegna near the Trevi Fountain. The collection on view here includes a Raphael fresco, a Rubens, three paintings attributed to Titian plus the only picture in Rome by Piazetta. A tour of this specialised gallery should take no more than half an hour.
Open: Monday, Wednesday, Friday, and last Sunday of each month 10.00–13.00 hrs. Admission charge.

◆
ANTIQUARIUM FORENSE - PALATINO
Piazza S Maria Nova 53
This museum houses archaeological finds of ancient Rome. At the time of writing it is under restoration, so check by telephone (679 0333) whether or not it is open to visitors.
Open: daily 09.00–18.00 hrs in summer; 09.00–15.00 hrs in winter. Admission charge.

◆
ARA PACIS AUGUSTAE (ALTAR OF AUGUSTAN PEACE)
Via di Ripetta
After Augustus's victories in Gaul and Spain, the Senate erected this monument (consecrated in 13 BC) to celebrate peace. The main structure is of gleaming white Carrara marble, quite simply designed and raised on a pyramid of steps. In contrast, the surrounding screen is beautifully decorated with reliefs. There are two levels, the upper of figures, the lower of stylised flowering plants and acanthus leaves. Look particularly at the relief at the eastern end which shows the earth goddess Tellus with a swan, cow and lamb.
The upper frieze shows mythical historic scenes including Aeneas making a sacrifice (according to the experts, the finest portion). But it also shows a procession of important personages who attended the consecration ceremony including Augustus himself. Look closely and you

One of the city's best preserved triumphal arches, the Arch of Constantine

will see priests, members of the Imperial family and lictors with their rods. One elderly person is believed to be Agrippa and the ladies represented are Augustus's wife, Livia, his daughter Julia and his niece Antonia. One of the three children portrayed is usually identified as the future Emperor Claudius. The altar was renovated in 1938.
Open: Tuesday to Saturday, 09.00–13.30 hrs, Sunday, 09.00–13.00 hrs. From April to October, also open Tuesday and Saturday, 15.30–19.00 hrs. Admission charge.

◆
ARCO DI CONSTANTINO (ARCH OF CONSTANTINE)
Piazza del Colosseo
This triple arch, one of the last of Ancient Rome's great monuments, was erected in 315 to commemorate the emperor's victory over Maxentius in 312 at the Milvian Bridge. It is apparent, however, that the arts in 4th-century Rome were on the decline for the workmanship showing Constantine speaking to the Romans is inferior to earlier triumphal arches. Indeed, the best reliefs to be seen were in fact taken from those previous monuments to Trajan, Hadrian and Marcus Aurelius.

WHAT TO SEE

♦♦
ARCO DI SETTIMIO SEVERO (ARCH OF SEPTIMIUS SEVERUS)

Western end of the Roman Forum

An arch built in AD 203 to celebrate the emperor's victories, it is in architectural terms very influential. Many designers copied it and it was a favourite subject of French 18th-century artist, Hubert Robert (or Robert des Ruines as he was nicknamed).

♦♦
ARCO DI TITO (ARCH OF TITO)

Eastern end of the Roman Forum

This, Rome's oldest surviving triumphal arch, was erected on top of the Velia in AD 81 to commemorate Jerusalem's capture 11 years earlier. The site is superb and the view from here is a Roman classic. The reliefs represent the spoils of the temple, including the seven-branched golden candlesticks and the silver trumpets. Even today, many Jews refuse to walk through the arch, built to glorify their tragedy.

♦
AURELIAN WALL

Aurelian and Probus erected this impressive wall between 272 and 279 and an amazingly large proportion of it remains visible and in good condition. Built to keep out the Alemanni whom Aurelian defeated, the wall took in all seven of the famous hills and was massively buttressed. It was 12 miles (19

Portions of the Aurelian Wall stand remarkably intact

km) in circumference and had 18 main gates and 381 towers. The best places to see it are at Porta San Sebastiano and along Via Campania, east of Porta Pinciana.

◆
AVENTINE HILL

One of Rome's original seven hills, this hill rises south of the Palatine Hill and from the Parco di Sant'Alassio, with views across the Tiber towards Trastevere and St Peter's. There are several churches worth seeing on Aventine (see page 67) but the main feature is Piazza dei Cavalieri di Malta, a square designed in the 18th century by famous engraver Piranesi, with cypress trees, small obelisks and trophies of arms – almost resembling one of the artist's own drawings. Peek through the keyhole of the door leading into the Knights' Priory on the right and you will see one of Rome's most exceptional views – the dome of St Peter's framed by the avenue of trees.

◆
BASILICA AEMILIA
Foro Romano

This ruined building is to the right as you enter the Forum and is the ideal illustration of how a market was changed into a meeting place. In the early part of the 5th century, this site was a row of butchers' shops which were gradually taken over by money changers, in their turn concealed by the portico built on the Forum side of the basilica.

The basilica was said by Pliny to be one of the world's most beautiful buildings. Built in 179 BC, the money changers were not sent away but concealed by a portico – which was reconstructed several times after fires. What you see today is the building after Alaric's sacking of Rome in AD 410.

◆◆
BASILICA DI S AGNESE
off Via Nomentana on the Via S Agnese

Possibly built by Constantine the Great's granddaughter, Constantia who lived in Rome between 337 and 350, to house the tomb of St Agnes martyred in 304, the site of the basilica may seem curious as it was built into the catacombs in which St Agnes was buried. The church you see today was built by Honorius I (625–38) over that founded by Constantia and has managed to preserve the air of a very ancient place of Christian worship, despite several restorations.

A highlight for sightseers is the superb 7th-century golden mosaic which portrays a young St Agnes in Byzantine dress flanked by the popes who built the church. The statue of St Agnes on the altar is a 16th-century piece of work in alabaster, beneath which lie her remains and those of St Emerentiana who was stoned to death when found praying by St Agnes's tomb.

Each year on 21 January, two lambs are blessed in this church and taken to the Pope for further blessing before being handed over to Trastevere nuns who spin and weave their wool into a bishop's vestment called the *pallium*.

◆◆
BASILICA DI S CLEMENTE
Piazza di S Clemente Via di S Giovanni in Laterano
Since 1667 the Irish Dominicans have been taking care of this ancient and appealing basilica and are always delighted to explain the complex history of what are three successive places of Christian worship, built one on top of the other between the 1st and 12th centuries.
The lowest level was originally a 1st-century mansion belonging to an early Christian. It was here that archaeologists discovered the remains of a *mithraeum* – a gathering place for a popular pagan cult around the time of Christ. Mithraism, pagan though it was, was a very moral religion which stressed loyalty and fidelity. Some think it influenced the development of Christianity.
The upper church features one of the most perfect medieval interiors to be seen in Rome. Beneath it the 19th-century martyr's tomb is said to contain the relics of St Clement and St Ignatius.
The magnificent blue, green and gold mosaic in the semi-dome is one of the finest pieces of workmanship in the whole church and may possibly incorporate stone fragments from the 4th-century church's original. Among the

The Vassallettos' exquisite cloister at San Giovanni in Laterano

other art treasures are the frescos in the side chapel of St Catherine of Alexandria (15th-century), attributed to Masolino da Panicale.

◆◆◆
BASILICA DI S GIOVANNI IN LATERANO
Piazza S Giovanni in Laterano
This is *the* cathedral church of Rome, alongside what was the papal residence for hundreds of years prior to the 14th century. It was originally built in the 4th century over

Imperial army barracks, and if it does not show its age it is because it has been so often rebuilt. Vandals practically destroyed the first building, an 8th-century earthquake ruined the second and it was twice burnt down in the 14th century. By the time Borromini was commissioned to carry out his restoration in 1646, there was little of the original structure to work with. The main façade as you see it today was the work of Alessandro Galilei in 1735, inspired as you can tell by St Peter's, and adorned by gigantic statues which have become a city landmark – visible from as far away as the Janiculum (see page 48). The

celebrated central antique bronze doors were brought here from the Senate House in the Forum – the *curia Iulia*; the door on the extreme right only opens during a Holy Year. On a pillar just inside is a fragment from Giotto's fresco showing Boniface VIII proclaiming that very first Holy Year in 1300. A little further on, against a pillar, is a monument to Pope Sylvester II (999–1003). The monument itself is recent (1909) but it incorporates an inscription which may have been part of Sylvester II's original tomb – and, it is said, just before the death of a pope it sweats and makes a sound like rattling bones.

WHAT TO SEE

Do not miss the papal altar, which contains a wooden table at which St Peter is believed to have celebrated Mass.

A small door at the end of the left aisle leads to the Cloisters, the most beautiful examples of Cosmatesque (mosaic) art anywhere in Rome. Executed by Vassalletto and his son in multi-coloured marble and gold, they were built between 1222 and 1230 and are quite exquisite, best viewed from the garden.

Next to the Basilica the Baptistry occupies the site of the baths of the 'House of Fausta' (Constantine's second wife). The octagonal building as you see it was built in Sixtus III's reign (434–440) when baptism was by total immersion. Four chapels surround the Baptistry: in that dedicated to St John are the famous bronze musical doors, believed to have come from the Baths of Caracalla.

Across the piazza is the Scala Santa (Holy Staircase), all that remains of the old Lateran palace, destroyed by Sixtus V in 1586 when he built the present Palazzo Laterano. By tradition, the Scala Santa was said to be those stairs in Pontius Pilate's Jerusalem residence ascended by Christ and brought to Rome by Constantine's mother, St Helena, and devout Catholics still climb them on their knees. They lead to the Sancta Sanctorum (Holy of Holies) or Chapel of S Lorenzo, once the popes' private chapel in the old palace.

The chapel is kept locked but you can peer through the grille at the many valuable relics, the most notable being a silver adorned picture of Christ which hangs above the altar – the *acheiropoieton* (not painted by human hands).

In the middle of Piazza di S Giovanni in Laterano stands Rome's oldest and tallest obelisk, dating from the 15th century BC when it stood in front of the Temple of Ammon in Thebes (Egypt). Constantius II brought it to Rome in AD 357 where it was placed in the Circus Maximus. It was found there in three pieces in 1587, removed by Sixtus V as an ornamental hub for his new road network.

Open: Basilica daily from 07.00–19.00 hrs; the Cloisters

One of the immense statues inside San Giovanni – the city's cathedral

from 09.00–18.00 hrs but closed lunchtime; the Baptistry from 08.00–12.00 and 15.00–18.00 hrs; the Scala Santa from 06.00–12.00 and 14.30–19.00 hrs.

◆◆
BASILICA DI SS GIOVANNI E PAOLO
Piazza di SS Giovanni e Paolo
The foundations of this church are thought to date from the 4th century, built by the senator Pammachius, on the site where St John and St Paul were martyred. They had been military officers under the first Christian Emperor Constantine before retiring to a private life, but were recalled into service by the emperor's pagan successor, Julian the Apostate in 360. When they refused to sacrifice to a pagan god, they were murdered here in their own home.
Excavations under the church have revealed two 2nd- and 3rd-century Roman houses which amazingly were used for burial (unusual within city limits). Several graves and tombs were discovered, as well as paintings, confirming that the saints' martyrdom really did take place here.

◆◆
BASILICA DI S LORENZO FUORI LE MURA (ST LAWRENCE OUTSIDE THE WALLS)
Piazzale S Lorenzo, Campo Verano
S Lorenzo (St Lawrence) was martyred in 258 during the rule of Emperor Valerian. Like many other early Christians he was buried in the catacombs.

After Constantine built a basilica over the site giving access to the saint's tombs, several popes were buried in the same catacombs. In the 5th century Sixtus III remodelled the sanctuary, but between 579 and 590 Pelagius II erected an entirely new basilica, which now serves as the chancel. Note the 6th-century mosaic portraying Pelagius offering Christ a model of his church. Additions were made to Pelagius's work by Pope Honorius II in the 13th century – these now serve as the nave. He also redecorated St Lawrence's tomb, enclosed in a crypt-like chapel beneath the main altar. The enormous Campo Verano cemetery surrounds S Lorenzo; since 1830 Catholics who die in Rome (with the exception of the pope, royalty and certain other people) have been buried here.

◆
BASILICA DI S MARCO
Piazza di S Marco
This is the Venetians' church in Rome, dedicated to their patron saint, St Mark, who is said to have written his Gospel while staying in a house on the slopes of the Capitol. It is equally dedicated to his namesake, St Mark, who was pope in 336, and the church's foundations certainly date from this time. The pope's relics lie under the main altar along with those of St Abdon and St Señnen.
The first church was the earliest Roman parish church to be built on the lines of a

classical basilica and incorporated a 3rd- to 4th-century mosaic floor, perhaps part of a Christian meeting place. A second church was built above it in the 6th century and the existing building in the 9th century by Pope Gregory IV.

Most of the present interior dates from the 17th and 18th centuries, but the lovely gilded ceiling and Renaissance portico belong to Paul II's time. Note the inscription on the right hand wall of the portico's ground floor – that of Borgia Pope Alexander VI's mistress, Vanozza Cattanei, mother of his three children.

◆◆
BASILICA S MARIA MAGGIORE
Piazza S Maria Maggiore
Situated on Esquiline Hill, this great patriarchal basilica is one of the most important

places of pilgrimage in the city. It has another title – Basilica Liberiana or Santa Maria delle Neve, but it was built by Sixtus III (432–40), not by Pope St Liberius (353–66) as legend would have us believe. That is not to say Liberius did not build a basilica on this same hill, though it has long vanished – and it is with that (not S Maria Maggiore) that the dream vision of the Virgin commanding the building of a church by creating a midsummer snowfall, should be associated. However, it was the Council of Ephesus's findings that inspired Sixtus to dedicate his church to the Virgin Mary (whose cult was to become so popular). He probably chose the site for the practical reason that many Roman women still frequented

Magnificent S Maria Maggiore dominates the Esquiline Hill

a temple of the mother-goddess Juno Lucina (on the same hill), and his aim was to substitute a Christian cult for a pagan one.

The basilica's exterior, almost completely 18th-century, remodelled by Ferdinando Fuga, hardly gives you an idea of the wealth inside. Thirty-six mosaic panels above the architrave represent Old Testament scenes, almost all dating from the time of Sixtus III. Easier to see are those gold and richly coloured mosaics in the triumphal arch depicting the main events of Christ's childhood.

Much of this basilica's glory lies with these mosaics, but three other things have added to the fame: the Oratory of the *presepio* (or Christmas crib) has been documented as early as the 7th century – a small chapel designed to resemble the Nativity grotto in Bethlehem which stood outside the church. When the oratory collapsed, mosaics and marbles fragmented and only a few statues were saved. Those of St Joseph, the three kings, the ox and the ass, all part of Arnolfo's original stable scene, survived and remain among S Maria Maggiore's most superb features. If you would like to see them, ask in the sacristy for someone to open the door to the underground grotto.

Beneath the high altar is a statue of Pius IX kneeling before a reliquary of the holy crib. The latter is only exposed once a month (on the 25th) and on Christmas Eve is carried solemnly around the basilica. The relic is believed to date sometime between the 7th and 9th centuries and is curiously inscribed in Greek.

The other major treasure is in the ornately adorned Pauline Chapel, built in 1611. Almost all Rome's sculptors of the time made their contribution, among them Pietro Bernini. You cannot help but be overawed by the richness of the main altar embedded with jasper, agate, amethyst and lapis lazuli. At the centre is the celebrated *acheiropoieton* (supposed not to have been painted by human hands) picture of the *Madonna and Child* (possibly 8th-century). Every August 5, white flower petals flutter from this chapel's dome in commemoration of Liberius's vision and legendary snowfall.

◆◆
BASILICA DI S PAOLO FUORI LE MURA
Via Ostiense

It is tragic that an 1823 fire necessitated the reconstruction of this great basilica which had previously remained almost unchanged from when it was begun in the 5th century. Its location, ouside the city walls, had helped protect it and before the disastrous fire it was one of Rome's best decorated churches, full of handsome frescos and mosaics. In its rebuilt neo-classical form it lacks warmth and atmosphere and little was salvaged of its original embellishments, though post-fire gifts for it included

WHAT TO SEE

alabaster columns from Egypt and lapis lazuli for the altar from Tsar Nicholas I of Russia. The very badly damaged bronze doors, once richly inlaid with silver and made in Constantinople in 1070 can again be seen in the 13th-century cloister, which miraculously escaped unscathed from the fire. *Open:* Cloisters 09.00–13.00 and 15.00–18.00 hrs.

◆◆◆
BASILICA DI S PIETRO
Piazza S Pietro
For almost everybody, St Peter's is the jewel in Rome's crown. After years of enormous undertaking, reconstructing and enlarging Constantine's original church, St Peter's as you see it now was consecrated in 1626. That first basilica on the traditional burial site of St Peter was consecrated in AD 326 but by the 16th century it was considered unsafe and Julius II commissioned the architect Bramante to start afresh in 1506. Bramante died before his plan for a magnificent church in the form of a Greek cross could be realised, and subsequently several architects, including Michelangelo, then 71, had a hand in the final design, which ended up in the form of a Latin cross. Carl Maderno's façade almost eclipses the beautiful dome (almost entirely Michelangelo's work and best viewed from the back, in the Vatican Gardens). Above Bernini's portico is the 'benediction loggia' from

which the Pope gives his blessings. Of the five great entrance doors, that to the right is opened only every 25 years during a 'Holy Year'. The central bronze doors took Antonio Filarete 12 years to complete (1433–45) and he 'signed' his doors on the back, portraying himself and his assistants having fun doing the work. You will also note Bernini's Scala Regia (Royal Staircase), an entrance which is only rarely opened. Before going inside, glance back to what remains of Giotto's famous mosaic of the Navicella above the central portal, showing Christ walking on the water and below him, scarcely distinguishable, the 13th-century mosaic's donor, Cardinal Stefaneschi. Inside you cannot fail to be impressed by the size and grandeur – there is so much gold, marble and mosaic work some may even find the atmosphere oppressive. If you want to compare dimensions with other famous cathedrals look at the floor of the central nave where they have been marked.

St Peter's most famous work of art is to be found in the chapel immediately to the right of the entrance. This is Michelangelo's *Pietà*, sculpted when he was 25 years of age and the only piece he ever signed. It stands under a spotlight and is (since a frenzied hammer attack in 1972) protected by bullet proof glass. Another celebrated statue is that of *St Peter Enthroned*, seen at the end of

St Peter's and Via delle
Conciliazone at sunset

the nave on the right, near the
Papal altar. Made of bronze, it
is attributed to Arnolfo di
Cambio (13th century): note
how the statue's right foot has
been worn by the touches of
countless reverent pilgrims.
Much of the baroque interior is
the work of Bernini, including
the great bronze *baldacchino*
centrepiece – a canopy which
took 10 years to finish and is
raised above the papal altar. It
is dedicated to the Barberini
Pope Urban VIII, who had
bronze removed from the
Pantheon's portico to make it
and insisted on his heraldic
bees being incorporated in the
design of the supporting
columns.

The *sacre grotto* or crypt
marks St Peter's last resting
place and is almost all that
remains of the old basilica.

Bernini's bronze altar canopy is the centrepiece of the ornate baroque interior

Here are the tombs of many popes. Beneath the papal altar a heavy gilded grille conceals the 6th-century *Niche of Pallia* – the original if much restored mosaic of Christ.

Excavation work in the 1940s under and around the shrine of St Peter brought to light a pre-Constantine necropolis as well as the simple monument believed to be St Peter's burial place. An eyewitness in AD 200 had described an *aedicula* (pavilion) containing St Peter's tomb, and Vatican archaeologists confirmed its existence, though there was clear evidence of destruction. The only relics found were some bones, said to be human and declared to be those of St Peter. A guided tour of the pagan tombs is possible, but only with advance appointment by applying to the Prefettura Casa Pontificia, Città del Vaticano, 00120 (giving language spoken, length of visit to Rome, address and telephone number). They are certainly worth seeing, for many of the tombs are sumptuously decorated with frescos, terra cotta and stucco reliefs. They were mostly built between 125 and 200 as burying places for the well-to-do.

Bernini designed the *Cattedra di S Pietro* surrounds and bronze throne that encase an ancient ivory-decorated wooden chair supposedly used by the apostle. The Treasury now contains a history and art museum – a fascinating collection of sacred relics, and you can climb to the dome by lift and then up 537 steps, for one of Rome's most splendid views.

Open: Basilica 07.00–19.00 hrs (18.00 in winter); Treasury 09.00–18.00 hrs (16.30 in winter) admission charge; Dome 08.00–18.15 hrs (16.45 in winter).

◆
BASILICA DI S SEBASTIANO
Via Appia Antica
The original basilica was built in the 4th century but acquired its name in the Middle Ages and its present day

appearance in the 17th century when Cardinal Scipione Borghese commissioned Flavio Ponzio to restore it. Work was completed by Giovanni Vasanzio, architect of the Villa Borghese, who is also said to have carved the wooden ceiling. The main feature is a recumbent statue of St Sebastian by Antonio Giorgetti in a left-hand chapel over the original tomb below. In the opposite chapel in a reliquary is a stone purported to bear Christ's footprints. A visit here is usually combined with that of the Catacombs of St Sebastian.

◆
BATHS OF CARACALLA
Via delle Terme di Caracalla
At one time these *terme* (baths) were the most luxurious in Rome. They were begun by Septimius Severus in 206 but are more associated with his son, Caracalla, who inaugurated them 11 years later. More than 1,500 people could bathe here at one time, enjoying the ancient equivalent of what we today term as saunas, Turkish steam baths, hot tubs and plunge pools. Again, the complex was more than a place to get clean – it was a social centre with gardens, a stadium, libraries, lecture rooms and shops. They remained functioning until the Goths cut the aqueducts' water supply in the 6th century. Enough of the ruins survive today to provide a handsome stage for open air summer operas. If you can, try to see Verdi's *Aida* here – there is room on stage for a cast of

hundreds, plus horses and chariots.
Open: Tuesday–Saturday 09.00–16.00 hrs; Sunday, Monday 09.00–13.00 hrs.

◆◆◆
BATHS OF DIOCLETIAN
Piazza della Repubblica
Maximian began building these baths (the largest in Rome) in AD 298 but they were completed by Diocletian some seven years later. Like most buildings of Ancient Rome, they were designed on a monumental scale to cover 32 acres with marble-faced walls that housed baths for 3,000 with a *calidarium* (hot bath), *tepidarium* (temperate bath) and *frigidarium* (cold bath). As with all old bathing establishments, there were

The Lancelotti Discus Thrower in the Museo Nazionale Romano

WHAT TO SEE

Aphrodite, goddess of love, rising from the waves

libraries, exercise rooms, gardens and a vast collection of artwork, so it is perhaps appropriate that much of the complex today is occupied by the Museo Nazionale Romano. Before entering the museum, take a look at the **Church of Santa Maria degli Angeli**, which in 1561 Pius IV commissioned Michelangelo to convert from the central hall of the frigidarium. He did so with great taste and respect for such classical ruins, which is more than did his 18th-century successor, Vanvitelli. The latter moved the main door to the calidarium where it is now, incorporated the tepidarium and turned Michelangelo's nave (once the frigidarium) into a vast transept.

The **Museo Nazionale Romano** was founded in 1889 as a repository for all antique and meritorious artwork discovered in Rome. There are countless important items here, but many remain in storage. At the time of writing restoration work is taking place so you may wish to check what is, and what is not, open to the public (tel: 460 856).

If open, one of the major features is the Ludovisi Collection, of which the most famous item is the Greek 'throne' dating from the 5th century BC and showing a breathtaking relief of Aphrodite, goddess of love, being borne from the waves: it is one of the most beautiful pieces of sculpture in Rome. Another masterpiece is the *Niobid*, also the original work of a 5th-century BC Greek sculptor. It portrays one of Niobe's 14 children attempting to remove an arrow shot at her by Artemis. Look also for the *Venus of Cyrene* representing the goddess Aphrodite, believed to be a copy of a Greek bronze though the actual date of the work has never been clarified. It was discovered by accident by two army officers after a storm in 1913.

Another celebrated work of art in this museum, is the *Girl of Anzio*, a particularly lovely statue also discovered after a storm which carried away part of the ruined wall of the villa of Anzio in 1878. It is thought she represented some kind of sacrificial servant and the statue's appeal is in both her look of concentration and in the sculpting of her dress. Look too for the Anzio *Apollo* and the Lancelotti *Discus Thrower*, the best preserved copy of a Greek original, probably made in the 2nd century AD. To appreciate the old Roman art of interior decoration, you should try to see the frescoed garden room from Empress Livia's villa, discovered in 1863, and skilfully removed from the villa to the museum to prevent its being ruined by damp.
Open: Tuesday to Saturday 09.00–14.00 hrs, Sunday 09.00–13.00 hrs. Admission charge.

◆
BORGO
A district immediately east of St Peter's, flanking the wide thoroughfare of Via della Conciliazione, but still boasting typically medieval streets. Half way up Via della Conciliazione are two old palaces: the **Palazzo Torlonia**, built between 1496 and 1504 – the work of architect Andrea Bregno and prior to the Reformation, the seat of Henry VIII's Embassy to the Holy See. Opposite, the

15th-century **Palazzo dei Penitensieri**, originally built for a cardinal, is now the Hotel Columbus. Off the Borgo Santo Spirito you will see the **Ospedale Santo Spirito**, part 15th-century building, part modern hospital; the **Palazzo del Commendatore**, a 16th-century residence for the hospital's director; and the **Church of Santo Spirito in Sassia**, a fine Renaissance building.

◆◆
CAMPO DEI FIORI
This large square is best known for its picturesque fruit and flower market. Literally translated, its name means 'field of flowers' and before 1600 it was the centre of a select residential and business district. After 1600 it was used as a place for executions.

◆
CAMPO MARZIO (CAMPUS MARTIUS)
Literally translated, it means 'the field of Mars' and in ancient times was a vast flat plain bordered by the city's monumental baths and theatres, ideal for horse and chariot racing, ball games, gymnastics and military exercises. When the Goths besieged Rome, cutting the aqueducts in 537, the populace was forced to leave their now waterless higher residential district and build hovels to live in around the great monuments of the Campus where water was more easily obtainable. This led to the Campus becoming the main centre of Rome for many centuries.

WHAT TO SEE

◆◆◆
CAPITOLINE HILL
Piazza del Campidoglio
It was the most famous of
Rome's seven hills – both the
seat of power and the
sanctuary for Ancient Rome.
Here stood the Temple of
Jupiter where the Senate held
its first session each year, now
lost save for some of the grey
stone blocks that formed part
of the podium to be seen as
you enter the Passaggio del
Muro Romano. Here, too, stood
the Citadel and the Temple of
Juno Moneta. Much of what
you see today was redesigned
by Michelangelo, and though
the **Palazzo Senatorio** is the
official seat of the municipality,
the Capitol is no longer the
city's political centre, but
instead a museum showplace.
It is reached via the elegant
cordonata, a gentle ramp
originally designed by
Michelangelo for Emperor
Charles V's triumphal entry
into Rome in 1536. In the
central piazza should be
standing the most famous
equestrian bronze survivor of
the ancient world, that of
Marcus Aurelius but it has
been removed for restoration.
Facing each other across the
square are the Palazzo Nuovo
and Palazzo dei Conservatori,
which together form the
Capitoline Museum, holding
the world's oldest and finest
public collection of works of
art, started by Pope Sixtus IV
and continually enlarged. A
third palace (the Cafarelli or
Museo Nuovo), reached
through the Conservatori, is
also part of the museum. Note

*Piazza del Campidoglio, awaiting
the return of the restored bronze
statue of Marcus Aurelius*

the fountain in the courtyard,
decorated by an immense
river god known as Marforio,
one of the 'talking statues'. For
centuries, such statues as this
played a role in political satire,
and papal affairs. Epigrams
and grafitti, written on cards,
were hung around their necks
for the general public to see
and read. The Palazzo Nuovo
contains many of the oldest
pieces in the collection, the
Capitoline Venus, a Roman
copy of a 2nd-century BC
original; the *Dying Gaul*, a
copy of a 3rd-century Greek
bronze; and the *Marble Faun*.
In the courtyard of the Palazzo
dei Conservatori are the
remains of a colossal statue of
the Emperor Constantine,

found in the basilica beside the
Forum.

Another great treasure in this
part of the museum (upstairs) is
the *Capitoline Wolf,* an
Etruscan bronze dating from
the end of the 6th century BC,
to which the twins, Romulus
and Remus were added in
1509. Many distinguished
paintings are also on display,
including *Baptism of Christ* (an
early Titian); Rubens' version
of *Romulus and Remus
Suckled by the She-Wolf*; and
Van Dyck's *Double Portrait of
the Painters Lucas and
Cornelius de Wael.* In another
hall, the *Rape of the Sabines* is
one of several important
narrative paintings by Pietro
da Cortona.
Open: daily except Monday
09.00–13.30 hrs, Tuesday and
Saturday also 17.00–20.00 hrs.
Admission charge.

◆◆◆
CASTEL SANT'ANGELO
Lungotevere Castello
It is almost impossible to miss
this Rome landmark, although
only the circular mound which
forms the base remains from
the original structure begun in
AD 130 by Emperor Hadrian,
intended as his mausoleum,
and completed in AD 139, a
year after his death, by his
successor Antoninus Pius. A
spiral ramp inside leads to a
second tier, the Imperial tomb,
where the urns containing the
ashes of emperors were kept.
The Castello remained a
mausoleum until Caracalla's
death at the beginning of the
3rd century when it became a
fortress, the Citadel of Rome.
Its name stems from a vision of
Pope Gregory the Great, who,
while on his way to St Peter's
in 590, saw an angel sheathing
a sword, above the Citadel,
signifying the end of the
plague. A chapel was
promptly built on the spot and
the fortress renamed, though
the bronze statue of St Michael
crowning the battlements was
added as recently as 1753.
In 847 Leo IV enclosed the
Borgo and Vatican within walls
and turned the fortress into a
citadel-cum-residence where
subsequent popes dwelt from
time to time for security. A
covered walkway was built to
link the Castel with the Vatican
by Alexander VI in the 15th
century and Pope Clement VIII
managed to escape along it
during the 1527 sack of Rome.
In the 16th century, under Paul
III, the interior was decorated
and the marble angel by

WHAT TO SEE

Raffaello de Montelupo (now in the Cortile di Onore) was placed at the summit. For many years, during the Renaissance period, the Castel was used as a prison and then as a papal palace. It was opened as a museum in 1933. There are four floors to visit, including the Papal Apartments, where valuable collections of paintings, furniture and tapestries are on view as well as an exceptional collection of arms and armour in the prison section, some of which date back to the 7th

Built as Hadrian's mausoleum, Castel Sant'Angelo is now a museum

century BC. The Chapel of Leo X is kept locked, but it is worth looking at, as it is one of Michelangelo's lesser known works. The Papal Apartments include superb frescos – *The Angel of Justice* by Perin del Vaga, grotesques frescoed for Paul III in 1547 in the adjacent Hall of Apollo, and the triptych by Taddeo Gaddi in a small room beyond. On the third floor, the Loggia of Paul III was designed by Raffaello da Montelupo and Antonio da Sangallo the Younger and leads to the open Gallery of Pius IV, a marvellous vantage point to overlook the city. From the Loggia of Julius II,

designed by Bramante, you can see the Ponte Sant'Angelo and from the terrace at the summit of the citadel, there are splendid views all round, particularly of St Peter's.
Open: Monday 14.00–19.30 hrs; Tuesday, Wednesday, Thursday, Friday, Saturday 09.00–14.00 hrs; Sunday 09.00–13.00 hrs. Admission charge.

◆◆◆
CATACOMBS

No one is really sure how many miles of underground galleries there are around Rome, but one calculation is that there are 500 miles (800

km) of catacombs used as burial places by the Ancient Romans, and later by the Christians. One of the better known early Christian cemeteries is the **Catacombs of St Callisto** or St Calixtus, accessible from the Via Appia Antica.
(*Open:* Thursday–Tuesday 08.30–12.00 and 14.30–17.30 hrs, to 17.00 hrs in winter. Closed Wednesday. Admission charge.)
These catacombs are among the largest in Rome, excavated to four levels and containing thousands and thousands of tombs of 3rd- and 4th-century Christians, though the official tour is naturally restricted to a small portion. The shelf-like compartments which form the burial niches are known as *loculi* and in some places there are as many as 12 to a tier each side of the narrow passageway. Chapels, called *cubicula*, have been carved out of the rock to hold families. They contain the Crypt of the Popes, where the tombstones of five popes who reigned between 230 and 283 may be seen. Next to this section is the Crypt of St Cecilia where it is believed the body of the young martyr was buried in 230. During the tour, the guide will undoubtedly point out some of the more interesting examples of graffiti – signs and symbols proclaiming Christian faith, simple Greek inscriptions and crudely scratched drawings.
Not far from the Catacombs of St Calixtus are the **Catacombs of St Sebastian**, also accessible

WHAT TO SEE

Follow in the footsteps of the Ancient Romans along the via Appia Antica

persecutions of 258 and remained here for some 40 years. If time and inclination permit, the **Catacombs of Priscilla** are also interesting. Entrance is by ringing the bell at the convent door at Via Salaria 430. (*Open:* Tuesday–Sunday 08.30–12.00 and 14.30–17.00 hrs. Closed Monday. Admission charge.) Benedictine nuns give guided tours of these catacombs which include the oldest known painting of the *Virgin and child with Isaiah*, dating from the 2nd century and found in a small *cubiculum* (chapel). Among the 2nd-century frescos is the earliest representation of the scene of *The Breaking of the Bread at the Last Supper*.

from the Via Appia Antica, entered to the right of the Church of St Sebastian. (*Open:* Friday–Wednesday 09.00–12.00 and 14.30–17.00 hrs. Closed Thursday. Admission charge.) Also on four levels, they were the only Christian cemetery to remain a place of pilgrimage right through the Middle Ages, despite the plague of malaria and marauding soldiers and bandits. It is believed that the bodies of the apostles, St Peter and St Paul were concealed here during Valerian's

◆
CIRCUS MAXIMUS
Via del Circo Massimo
Here the famous chariot races took place, some lasting as long as 15 days. Think of the film *Ben Hur* and you'll get the idea. Laps were recorded by moving large wooden eggs on the central spina or dividing barrier and winners and losers consoled themselves or celebrated in the shops and taverns that surrounded the circus. Later the arena was used for more barbaric and bloodthirsty extravaganzas, a water barrier separating the crowd from the wild animals that were slaughtered in their thousands.

A prototype for all the race courses in the ancient world, the Circus was started around 326 BC and the last games were held by Totila the Ostrogoth in

AD 549. Today all you can see is a grassy valley, the spina marked by a grassy bank with cypresses, and the Imperial box where the emperor and his court sat, which still juts out from Palatine Hill.

♦♦♦
COLOSSEUM
Piazza del Colosseo
A landmark ever since it was built in the 1st century, this amazing feat of engineering and architecture is *the* Roman monument for many people. Remarkably, it was raised on marshy ground and was originally a third of a mile in circumference. It was, of course, here that gladiators fought to the death, Christians were sent to the lions and other wild beasts battled with each other. Some 87,000 spectators could be seated to enjoy the gory spectacles which went on for days, shaded by a sailcloth awning. They could even win themselves a slave in an Imperial lottery. Not only did the Colosseum provide free, if cruel, entertainment for the masses; at one point it became a military fortress, at another it was used for bull fighting and at yet another as a gunpowder factory. In medieval and Renaissance times it was the main quarry for Rome's builders. Not until the 18th century was it protected from further pillage and destruction and decreed a place of pilgrimage. From the higher levels of the Colosseum there are wonderful views over the Forum, and the small museum

enables you to visualise the ordered seating arrangements and operation of grand scale events.
Open: daily 09.00–19.00 hrs (Wednesday to 13.00 hrs); in winter daily to 16.00 hrs. Admission charge for upper floor.

♦
ESQUILINE HILL
Nero's Golden House was built on one of this hill's summits, the Oppius, as well as the Baths of Trajan. Nowadays much of this area has become a public park. The other summit, the Cispius, is dominated by the Basilica of S Maria Maggiore.
Open: 09.00–13.00 and 15.00–18.00 hrs daily except Monday (in winter 10.00–16.00 hrs); Sunday 09.00–13.00 hrs.

♦
FONTANA DELLE API (FOUNTAIN OF THE BEES)
Piazza Barberini
At the corner of Via Vittorio Veneto stands one of Bernini's most delightful fountains, although it is not so conspicuous as many others in the city. It was constructed in honour (and in advance) of Urban VIII's 21st anniversary of accession to the pontificate in 1644.
Although the superstitious Romans chiselled away the last figure of the Roman numeral XXII, they were too late and Urban died eight days before his 22nd year began. The fountain splashes water into an open scallop shell where heraldic Barberini bees seem to be taking a drink.

WHAT TO SEE

◆
FONTANA DELL' ACQUA PAOLA (FOUNTAIN OF THE ACQUA PAOLA)
Via Garibaldi
Built for Pope Paul V by Giovanni Fontana in 1612 to celebrate the restoration of one of the aqueducts bringing water to the city, this one used marble and stone from Minerva's Temple. Its gushing sprays act as a backdrop for an unusual city view.

◆
FONTANA DELLA BARCACCIA (BARCACCIA FOUNTAIN)
Piazza di Spagna
This is the oldest architectural feature of the square, though no one is sure whether it is the work of Pietro Bernini or his more famous son Gian Lorenzo. The fountain makes use of the 'problem' of low water pressure (due to the lack of pressure in the Acqua Vergine) by its representation as an old boat sinking in an inadequate supply of water so it spits fitfully from prow and stern quite naturally.
According to legend, the fountain marks the spot where a boat was once stranded when the Tiber overflowed its banks.

◆◆
FONTANA DEI FIUMI (FOUNTAIN OF THE FOUR RIVERS)
Piazza Navona
Probably the most famous of Gian Bernini's fountains, this one was commissioned by Innocent X in 1648 to make the approach to Palazzo Pamphilj

more impressive, and was unveiled in 1651. The four rivers represented are the Nile, the Ganges, the Danube and the Plate. The statue of the Nile has its face covered not only to allude to the river's unknown source at the time, but also to obscure from its view Borromini's façade of the church of S Agnese. Similarly, the statue of The Plate raises its hand as if to stop the church falling down.
Bernini also rearranged the **Fountain of the Moor** (Fontana del Moro) at the southern end of the same piazza by adding the central figure to the triton setting sculpted by Giacomo della Porta in 1575, though he had nothing to do with **Neptune Fountain** (Fontana del Nettuno) at the piazza's northern end, which was completed in 1878.

◆◆◆
FONTANA DI TREVI (TREVI FOUNTAIN)
Piazza di Trevi
Rome's best known fountain is very big and fills a very small space tucked away among small back streets. Water passes along an aqueduct, called the Acqua Vergine (Virgin Spring), originally built by Emperor Agrippa in 19 BC and is the creation of Nicola Salvi, completed in 1762, although planned over a century before by Bernini. It is a fantastic waterscape of gods, goddesses, tritons and horses emerging from sculpted rocks amid cascades of water. The fountain probably takes its name from the three streets (tre via) which meet at this

If you want to return to Rome, throw a coin into Bernini's fantastic Trevi Fountain

point, and although not the easiest place, near the junction of the Corso and Via del Tritone, to find on your own, it is well worth it. If you want to ensure a return visit to Rome, do not forget to throw in a coin, a custom made even more popular by the film *Three Coins in the Fountain*.

◆◆
FONTANA DEL TRITONE (FOUNTAIN OF TRITON)
Piazza Barberini
Unquestionably a Bernini masterpiece, first designed around 1637. The group comprises four dolphins supporting a large sea shell on which a seated Triton spurts water through a conch held to his mouth. It is made of travertine instead of the usual marble.

◆◆◆
THE FORUM
Via dei Fori Imperali
Called the Roman Forum to
distinguish it from later
Imperial fora, this was the
political, religious and
commercial centre of
republican Rome. It may be
useful to take in the general
layout first from the terrace in
Via del Campidoglio.
Remember that it developed
gradually over hundreds of
years after Romulus made
peace with the Sabine leader,
Titus Tatius in 753 BC when this
area was nothing more than a
marshy plain between the
Capitoline and Palatine hills.
As you enter the Forum today,
to your right are the remains of
the **Basilica Aemilia**, which

would have been used as a
general meeting place to do
business. The ruins as you see
them were the result of
Alaric's catastrophic sack of
Rome in AD 410.
Crossing the Argiletum you
will reach a small open space
called the **Comitium** from
where orators addressed the
people. The well preserved,
austere red brick building you
see was the **Curia** or Senate
House – the present structure
dating from Diocletian times.
Dominating the area is the
Arch of Septimius Severus,
erected in AD 203 as a highly
decorated triumphal arch.
To the left of the Arch of
Septimus Severus stand the
surviving granite columns of
the **Temple of Saturn**. The

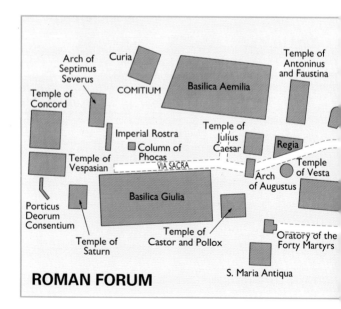

ROMAN FORUM

name was derived from the verb 'to sow' and the early Romans believed this god taught them agriculture and was therefore at this time responsible for their wealth. It was used as the state treasury and was also where the December Saturnalia festival (a sort of pagan Christmas) took place. The western branch of the Via Sacra (Sacred Way) leads to the square which is the Forum proper; in republican times the heart of the city's life, where religious ceremonies, sacrifices, elections and important funerals all took place.

Julius Caesar made a number of alterations including the moving of the **Imperial Rostra** whose remains you can just about make out and from where Mark Antony made his impassioned speech after Caesar's murder. He also began building the **Basilica Giulia**, which was completed by Augustus in AD 12. Very little of this is left, but the outline of it is clear; an enormous building that served as the central courthouse. The tall column, the **Column of Phocas**, however, was added much later in AD 608 in honour of that Byzantine usurper, Phocas, who had given the Pantheon to Pope Boniface IV. Augustus also erected the **Temple of Julius Caesar** in 29 BC when Caesar was officially deified, over the spot where his body was cremated, but

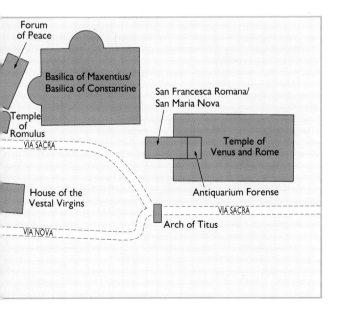

only traces of its existence can be seen.

Heading in an easterly direction you will arrive at the ruins of a small circular white marble temple, the **Temple of Vesta** and the **House of the Vestal Virgins**. The vestals' most important duty was to keep the sacred fire in the temple burning, for it symbolised the perpetuity of the State: extinction of the fire meant national catastrophe and certain punishment by the Pontifex Maximus whose official residence, the **Regia**, stood nearby. Its foundations can still be seen. The vestals led a simple, moral yet privileged life. If they broke their oath of 30 years virginity, they were buried alive, yet they enjoyed enormous influence and upon retirement received a generous dowry from the State. There has been a Temple of Vesta ever since there has been a Roman Forum, but the rebuilt remains you see today are fragments from the temple built by Septimius Severus and Julia Domna in AD 191. Turning left along a narrow paved street you will be confronted by three beautiful Corinthian columns, all that remain from the **Temple of Castor and Pollux**. Built in 484 BC, it was dedicated to the heavenly twins (brothers of Helen of Troy) for their divine intervention at the Battle of Lake Regillus, a victory which stopped any hopes of the Tarquin dynasty regaining sovereignty over Rome. According to legend, the

The immense remains of the Basilica of Maxentius, in the Forum

brothers were first seen watering their white steeds at the **Fountain of Jura**, still standing on the opposite side of the street. In ancient times it was a natural gathering place for gossip.

Retrace your steps past the Temple of Vesta and bear right into the main section of the Via Sacra. That splendid circular temple with porphyry columns and old bronze doors is the **Temple of Romulus** (4th-century), the son of Maxentius, who died young in 309. The vast brick and concrete

◆◆
THE FORUM (IMPERIAL)
Via dei Imperiali

Almost all of Rome's emperors were vain and egotistical enough to want to leave evidence of their wealth and power for subsequent generations and many of them built their own fora to the northwest of the original Roman Forum. Today these Imperial Fora are bisected by Mussolini's triumphal way, the Via dei Fori Imperiali and may be seen as follows:

The **Forum of Augustus** can be identified by the huge wall which separated it from the crowded Suburra quarter of the ancient city and includes the three columns of the **Temple of Mars Ultor** (Mars the Avenger). Augustus built this temple to commemorate his victory over Brutus and Cassius at the Battle of Philippi in 42 BC.

At the eastern end of the Forum of Augustus was the **Forum of Nerva**. These days modern streets and buildings cover it, but two impressive Corinthian columns are visible with a relief of Minerva (or Athene) between them. To the west of the Forum of Augustus stands the **Casa dei Cavalieri Rodi** (House of the Knights of Rhodes), the palace of the Knights of St John of Jerusalem. The view from the loggia takes in the whole of the Fori Imperiali, and from the atrium you can reach the Antiquarium of the Forum of Augustus whose sculptures include a particularly fine head of Jupiter.

structure is the **Basilica of Maxentius**, also known as the Basilica of Constantine, begun by the one and completed by the other.

The Sacred Way passes quite close to the church of **S Maria Nova**, which houses a lovely 12th-century mosaic of the *Madonna Enthroned with Saints*. Continue on to the **Arch of Titus** erected in 81 AD to commemorate the capture of Jerusalem 11 years previously. The high relief of its friezes make this a masterpiece.
Open: daily except Tuesday 09.00–18.00 hrs (winter to 15.00 hrs); Sunday 09.00–13.00 hrs. Admission charge.

The **Forum of Trajan** was perhaps the most impressive of the Imperial Fora and is reached via the lower level of Trajan's Markets, although it may also be seen from above. It was considered one of the world's wonders in its time, though it may be hard to visualise such splendour from what is left today. There is no sign of the great libraries and Temple of Trajan which once stood here, but at least one monument was left unscathed: **Trajan's Column**. Built in AD 113 to celebrate the Dacians' defeat, with 2,500 figures winding their way up the 125ft (38m) structure, it is full of information about Roman and barbaric arms and methods of warfare. Although no longer brightly coloured and gilded, the detailing is superb. Trajan's ashes were once contained inside the column and his statue topped it, to be replaced by that of St Peter in 1587.

◆
GIANICOLO (JANICULUM HILL)
near Porta S Pancrazio
Take the path past Gallori's **Garibaldi Monument** in Piazza del Gianicolo and you will have a wonderful view over the old city in the east. Guiseppe Garibaldi was one of the hero soldiers of modern Italy who fought against the French during the short-lived Roman Republic of 1849. It was on Janiculum Hill that the decisive battle took place, and when Italy became a state in 1870 **Gianicolo Park** was laid

out. The equestrian statue of Garibaldi itself dates from 1895 and the hill (not one of Rome's seven originals) takes its name from the god Janus.

◆◆
ISOLA TIBERINA (TIBER ISLAND)
Midstream in the River Tiber, with the Trastevere district on one side and Cenci on the other, is Tiber Island, linked to the mainland by two ancient bridges. It has a long association with the art of healing. The church of S Bartolomeo here may well have been built on the site of the Temple of Aesculapius (god of healing) which had been erected in thanks for the end of the plague of 291 BC. The sick sheltered here in the hope of getting well and they continued to do so in the Middle Ages when it was a church. It was here that Henry II's jester, Rahere, is said to have had a vision which resulted in the founding of St Bartholomew's Hospital in London. Even today, the massive modern hospital of the Fatebenefratelli is located on the island.

◆
KEATS-SHELLEY MEMORIAL
Piazza di Spagna 26
John Keats and his friend Joseph Severn lived in this small house to the right of the Spanish Steps and it was here that Keats died in a tiny room in 1821, aged only 25. A death mask on display shows his peaceful expression. Today, this house is a working library for students of Keats and

A peaceful library in the Piazza di Spagna: the Keats – Shelley Memorial

Shelley, who also died in Italy. *Open:* weekdays 09.00–13.00, 15.00–18.00 hrs. Admission charge.

◆◆
MERCATI TRAIANEI (TRAJAN'S MARKETS)
entrance from Via V Novembre
Part of Trajan's Forum complex designed by Apollodorus of Damascus in the early 2nd century, this well preserved shopping centre was accessible on two levels. You will enter via a great vaulted hall with rows of small stores ranged in tiers on either side, which probably sold speciality goods. At the far end, a staircase leads to the Via Biberatica (a medieval corruption of *pipera* – the

word for pepper, from which this street of spice shops took its name). More tiered shops overlook the Forum, linked by broad staircases, some original. In some of them you might see a small drain in the middle of the floor, showing that they would have sold oil or wine.
Open: Tuesday–Saturday 09.00–13.00 hrs; Tuesday, Thursday and Saturday also 16.00–19.00 hrs; Sunday 09.00–13.00 hrs (closed Monday). Admission charge.

◆◆
MONUMENTO VITTORIO EMANUELE II (MONUMENT TO VICTOR EMMANUEL II)
Piazza Venezia
Romans call it 'the wedding cake' and in many ways this gigantic mass of white Brescian marble does resemble one. It was built to celebrate the

unification of Italy, designed by Giuseppe Sacconi and unveiled in 1911. After World War I, the tomb of the unknown soldier was added to the first level by the Altare della Patria. Its scale is rather out of touch with Rome's surrounding treasures but the views from its top level over the city are spectacular.

◆◆
PALATINO (PALATINE HILL)
entrance through the Roman Forum
The Palatine, one of those original hills of Rome, has been called 'the cradle of Roman civilisation'. It is both historic and a pleasant, almost rustic, area to ramble in whether or not you are interested in classical ruins. If legend is to be believed, it was here that Romulus and Remus were suckled by the she-wolf and here, too, in 753 BC that the first city boundary lines were traced out.

The remains include those of the **House of Livia**, though it is doubtful whether this was the home where Augustus and his Empress dwelled. Tiberius was the first to build an imperial residence here, **Domus Tiberiana** of which some of the substructure is visible and some vaulted rooms have been preserved along the Clivus Victoriae. Caligula extended the domus towards the Roman Forum and built a bridge to connect it with the Capitol. Ruins of this later addition are known as the **Palace of Caligula**. On the eastern side of the domus is

Nero's famous **cryptoporticus**, a vaulted passage decorated with stuccoes. The most extensive ruins are those of the **Domitian Palace**, built at the end of the 1st century by Rabirius. It was a complex comprising the emperor's official residence, his private abode and a large stadium, a structure which entailed levelling much of the Palatine. Not much is to be seen of his private quarters, **Domus Augustana**, nor, for safety reasons, the **stadium**, though it is the most imposing relic. Best preserved ruins on the Palatine are those of the **Domus Severiana** or Palace of Septimius Severus, which include part of the baths he built. You will pass through them to reach the emperor's terrace or **Belvedere** from which there is a panoramic view. The **Farnese Gardens**, which were created in the first half of the 16th century by Vignola for Alexander Farnese, Pope Paul III's nephew, were Europe's earliest botanical gardens but only a fraction of them exist today.
Open: 09.00–18.00 hrs (in winter to 15.00 hrs); Sunday to 13.00 hrs (closed Monday). In combination with Roman Forum. Admission charge.

◆◆◆
PANTHEON
Piazza della Rotonda
Of all Rome's ancient monuments, this Temple of All the Gods, built by Hadrian in AD 125, is the best preserved. When it is floodlit at night, its

vast columns and huge concrete dome look their best. As old as it is, this is not the original Pantheon. That was built in 27 BC by Marcus Agrippa, hence the bold inscription on the pediment which modest Hadrian let be after a fire destroyed the rest. The Pantheon was saved from the fate of other structures by being given as a gift to Boniface IV by Byzantine Emperor Phocas in 608 and thus became a Christian church. On the Pope's orders, cartloads of martyred Christians' bones were removed from the catacombs and reburied here. It did not escape all desecration, for later popes and emperors stripped it of its gilded bronze and marble, though the great bronze doors are the originals. The jewel-covered statues of gods and goddesses have long since disappeared from their niches inside but restoration work gives some idea of how the interior might have looked. The Pantheon is the last resting place of several famous Renaissance artists, including Raphael, as well as the first two kings of modern Italy, Vittorio Emanuele II and Umberto I.
Open: Monday–Saturday 09.00–19.00 hrs; Sunday 09.00–13.00 hrs.

The tomb of King Umberto I in Hadrian's ancient Pantheon, where Raphael is also buried

◆
PIRAMIDE DI SESTIO (PYRAMID OF CESTIUS)
Porta S Paolo
Small by Egyptian standards, but high enough for Rome at 88 feet (28m), this pyramid was built as a tomb by a wealthy politician in 12 BC. According to the inscription, Caius Cestius used to supervise sacrificial banquets and the pyramid took 330 days to build. The monument would, of course, be one of the last things St Paul saw by the Ostian Way as he was led to his execution, since the Aurelian wall did not then exist.

◆
PONTE FABRICIO
The oldest bridge in the city (62 BC) at Tiber Island is better known as the Ponte dei Quattro

Capi or bridge of the four heads, from the four-headed Janus on the parapet.

◆◆
PONTE SANT'ANGELO

The most beautiful of Rome's old bridges, this one connects the city with Castel Sant'Angelo. Its three central arches are the ancient remnants of the original bridge, Pons Aelius, built by Hadrian in 133 which would have led to the family mausoleum. Bernini designed the statues of St Peter and St Paul and the ten angels in their variety of poses and the work was carried out by his pupils in 1668 to adorn the parapets.

◆
PORTA MAGGIORE

An imposing gateway built by Claudius in AD 52 at the intersection of Via Prenestina and Via Labicana. It was part of the Claudian aqueduct, concealing conduits of both the Aqua Claudia and the Anio Novus, later incorporated into the Aurelian Wall.

◆
PORTA PIA

An historic gateway commissioned by Pius IV in 1561 and built to Michelangelo's design, it was reconstructed between 1853 and 1861 by Virginio Vespignani and it was by breaches in the walls on either side of this gate that the armies of united Italy entered Rome in September of 1870. The building now houses the **Bersaglieri Museum** which contains military memorabilia.

◆
PORTA S SEBASTIANO

The best preserved gateway in the Aurelian Wall, behind the Arch of Drusus. First known as the Porta Capena when it was in the Servian Wall, it then became Porta Appia and was reconstructed in the early 5th century by Emperor Honorius and restored by Belisarius and Narses in the 6th century. The gate is flanked by two medieval towers and is best viewed from the Via Appia outside.

◆◆
PROTESTANT CEMETERY

Via Caio Cestio

Many famous people are buried in the older section of this cemetery. Most British visitors come to see the grave of the poet, John Keats, who died in 1821, and his friend Joseph Severn. In the new section, Percy Bysshe Shelley, Keats' fellow poet, is buried. He died of drowning in 1822 and was cremated on a beach. His friend Trelawney brought his heart to Rome and laid it to rest here. He himself was buried next to the poet 59 years later.

Open: daily 08.00–11.30, 15.20–17.30 hrs.

◆◆◆
SCALINATA DELLA TRINITA DEI MONTI
(SPANISH STEPS)

Piazza di Spagna

Meeting place, posing place, tourist landmark, the steps which lead from the square to the church of Trinità dei Monti were built between 1723 and 1726 by Francesco de Sanctis.

◆
TEATRO DI MARCELLO
(THEATRE OF MARCELLUS)
Via del Teatro di Marcello
Begun by Julius Caesar and completed by Augustus, this enormous 20,000-seat amphitheatre was dedicated in 13 BC to Caesar's nephew, Marcus Claudius Marcellus, who died aged 25. In the Middle Ages it was converted into a fortress and in the 16th century into a palace for the Savelli family by Peruzzi. It then became the Orsini Palace (named for the famous family who owned it for two centuries) and is now split into apartments Originally there were 41 arches in each of the two tiers (now there are only 12), and the small shops which had

grown up under the arches over the years were cleared by Mussolini. The three Corinthian columns left standing to the north of the building are the remains of the Temple of Apollo, first built in the 5th century BC and reconstructed in 34 BC.

◆◆◆
THE VATICAN
The Vatican is more than a city: it is the world's smallest independent sovereign state, established by the Lateran Treaty of 1929 and ruled by the Pope. The 108-acre area (less than a quarter of a square mile) on the right bank of the Tiber is completely self-sufficient, with its own civil and judicial systems, post office,

| 1 Musei del Vaticano | 3 Cappella Sistina | 5 Basilica di S. Pietro |
| 2 Cancello di S. Anna | 4 Portone di Bronzo | 6 Arco delle Campane |

bank, newspaper and radio station, railway station and supermarket. It is best known for the great Basilica of St Peter.

In ancient times the hill was known as Ager Vaticanus (near Nero's Circus) and was chosen as the site for a Christian basilica because it was believed to be St Peter's burial place. Emperor Constantine built the first basilica in the 4th century. The one you see dates from the 16th century.

There are three entrances to the Vatican City: through the

The colourful traditional uniform of the Vatican's Swiss Guard

Arch of Bells (Arco delle Campane), through the Bronze Gate (Portone di Bronzo), which is under the Bernini Colonnade, or through St Anne's Gate (Cancello di S Anna) in the Via di Porta Angelica. The Vatican Museum complex contains the world's largest collection of antique art and not even its highlights can be seen in one visit. The authorities do suggest colour coded tour routes, lasting between one-and-a-half to five hours should you care to follow them. Hurried visitors, for example, may head directly for the Sistine Chapel from the street entrance. However, because a one-way system operates, it is very difficult to backtrack if you miss something. Starting at the inner museum entrance of the Atrio dei Quattro Cancelli and climbing the Scala Simonetti, you will reach a long series of galleries leading eventually to the Sistine Chapel. Everyone will pass through the **Gallery of the Candelabra** (Galleria dei Candelabri) so named for its magnificent old marble candelabra, though it also contains important statues like the 2nd-century copy of *Diana of the Ephesians*. The beautiful tapestries at the far end of the gallery were designed by Raphael's pupils. Next we come to the **Gallery of the Maps** (Galleria delle Carte Geografiche) whose walls are frescoed with 16th-century maps, the work of Antonio Danti. Then to the small **Gallery of Pope Pius V**, where

Fra Angelico's triptych, one of thousands of treasures in the Vatican Museums

tapestries include 15th-century Belgian work. All four routes pass through the **Sobieski Room** with its Jan Metejko painting of Polish king John III Sobieski, and the **Room of the Immaculate Conception** where books and manuscripts are displayed. Only the two longer routes lead to **Raphael's Stanze**, four rooms comprising the private apartment of Julius II (he did not like the Borgia apartment), designed by Raphael. The two central rooms, the Stanza della Segnatura or study library, and the Stanza di Eliodoro (bedroom) are considered to contain the artist's finest work. From the last room of the Stanza (Sala di Constantino) you reach Sala dei Palfrenieri, mostly decorated in the 16th century. A door at the far right hand corner of this room leads to an often missed gem, the **Chapel of Nicholas V**. It is tiny but exquisite, painted by Fra Angelico between 1447 and 1449, showing scenes from the lives of St Stephen and St Lawrence.

Additionally, the longer routes take in the **Borgia Apartment** below Raphael's Stanze, taking its name from the second Borgia pope, Alexander VI, after his succession in 1492. He used the first floor suite of rooms (reconstructed by Nicholas V a little time before) as his personal apartment and commissioned Pinturicchio to do the fresco work. Nowadays, the apartment is the setting for displays of part of Pope Paul VI's collection of modern religious art. All tours end up in the **Sistine Chapel** (Capella Sistina), the Vatican's ultimate glory. Built for Sixtus IV towards the end of the 15th century, it was decorated by that period's greatest artists – Botticelli, Ghirlandaio, Pinturicchio and Signorelli. But it was Michelangelo's

WHAT TO SEE

painting of the huge ceiling between 1508 and 1512, and his masterpiece *The Last Judgment*, which have given this chapel its supreme status. Initially, Michelangelo had not been keen to take on the commission and indeed it proved an almost superhuman feat (for which he was paid little) to cover that 10,000 ft^2 (929 m^2) of space. The scenes tell the story of the Creation, the Fall and Noah, and while the unveiling of the ceiling drew the greatest praise, the gigantic composition of the Last Judgment, inaugurated in 1541, resulted in divided opinion as to its merit. Some saw it as a masterpiece, as we do today; others regarded it as offensive. By comparison with the joyful Renaissance-spirited ceiling, this is a powerfully sombre work showing a young beardless Christ in final judgment of humanity, including actual faces of Michelangelo's friends and enemies. The popes were not amused by so much nakedness and orders were given for draperies in 1564, later removed. Recent cleaning of the Sistine Chapel has shown the colours used in their clearer true shades. The **Vatican Library** is marked on all four tour routes and contains thousands of codices, manuscripts and early printed books. Some of the most beautiful and interesting are displayed in the Sala Sistina. You will find copies of Virgil's works dating from the 4th and 5th centuries; poems by

Michelangelo written in his own hand; a batch of love letters written by Henry VIII to Anne Boleyn. The collection grew over the centuries from the time Nicholas V started it in 1447 with 340 books.

The **Braccio Nuovo** (tour routes C and D) is a 19th-century addition or 'new wing' for the Chiaramonti Museum, built for Pius VII and containing classical statuary. One of the most imposing is a colossal figure of the *Nile*.

The **Egyptian Museum** (tour routes C and D) was the result of Gregory XVI's efforts in the early 19th century. Here are statues which are Roman imitations of Egyptian style

(many from Hadrian's Villa). The **Pio-Clementine Museum** (tour routes C and D) is named for the two 18th-century popes who assembled a magnificent collection of sculpture in an orderly way. Some of the greatest treasures are to be seen in the octagonal court, including *Apollo Belvedere*, once part of Julius II's collection, a handsome 2nd-century Roman copy of Leochares' 330 BC original. The museum also contains the legendary *Laocoon*, rediscovered in 1506 near

Henry VIII's love letters to Anne Boleyn are displayed in the Vatican Library

Nero's Golden House. The group represents one of Apollo's priests with his two sons struggling against two serpents. Made in Greek marble in the 2nd century BC it is the work of Agesander and his sons Athendorus and Polydorus of Rhodes. From ancient times it was considered one of the world's most wonderful pieces of sculpture.

The **Gregorian-Etruscan Museum**, founded by Gregory XVI in 1837 (on tour routes B and D) holds some of the world's best Etruscan artefacts, including an excellent collection of vases. There are also some Greek originals, notably the *Stele de Palestrita*, a 5th-century BC sepulchral relief.
Open: 09.00–16.00 hrs (in winter to 13.00 hrs). Closed Sunday and religious holidays. Admission charge.

◆◆◆
VILLA BORGHESE
Rome's second largest park was primarily created by Cardinal Scipione Borghese in the 17th century, inspired by Tivoli. It is easy enough to escape the roads that nowadays traverse the area, and enjoy the tranquility of the lake and tree-shaded walks. A bridge connects it to the Pincio Gardens and at the northern end is Rome's small zoo. The Borghese Gallery is housed in the building erected as a pleasure house for the Cardinal, the casino.
The Borghese's collection of artwork is second only to that found in the Vatican. Despite

Villa Borghese – tranquillity in the heart of the city

the fact that Napoleon forced the prince of his day to sell over 200 pieces from his collection to the Louvre, this remains full of masterpieces. The most famous piece is in the room to your right on the ground floor – the reclining figure of Pauline Bonaparte as *Venus* by Antonio Canova in 1804. Rumour has it that it was too lifelike for her husband, Camillo Borghese, who kept it locked up and only showed it to a select few.

Most of the sculpture is on the ground floor, with Bernini's

David, dominating Room II. Commissioned by Scipione, its face is said to be that of the young sculptor.

A feast of paintings in the first floor gallery includes the Raphaels in Room IX, of which the prime composition is the *Deposition* (1507), commissioned by Atlanta Baglioni in memory of her murdered son. Removal of over paint from the portrait of *An Unknown Man* revealed this as a Raphael not, as was long believed, a Holbein.

The Gallery is noted, too, for its Caravaggios in Room XIV. His realistic strokes bring life to *Madonna dei Palafrenieri* and to the fruit and leaves in *Sick Bacchus*, which like Goliath in his *David and Goliath* is reputed to be a self–portrait. Rubens's powerful *Deposition* is displayed in Room XV, but it is Titian's *Sacred and Profane Love* in the last of the Gallery's rooms that is most familiar to visitors, having been reproduced so often. It was painted around 1512 for the Aurelia family.

Open: 09.00–14.00 hrs; Sunday to 13.00 hrs (closed Monday).

◆◆
VILLA FARNESINA
Via della Lungara
This elegant Renaissance villa was built by Baldassare Peruzzi for Agostino Chigi in the early 16th century and it became the rendezvous for the celebrities of the day. Popes, diplomats and philosophers dined at Chigi's banquets in a setting decorated by Raphael and his pupils, including Giulio Romano, Sebastiano del Piombo and Sodoma. In 1579 Chigi was forced to sell the villa to the Farnese family, hence its present name. The Loggia of Psyche, now glassed in, would have given direct access to the garden and is decorated with garlands of fruit and flowers to give the impression of a summer pergola, whilst the ceiling depicts scenes from Psyche's life, completed in 1517. The loggia leading from this one – the Galatea, once also an open gallery – is certainly the work of Raphael himself, portraying Galatea driving a scallop-shell chariot and a team of dolphins. Before leaving the ground floor, look in at the small room at the other end of the Loggia of Psyche where an enchanting decorative frieze was added by Peruzzi. Upstairs, in the Hall of Perspectives, the villa's grand living room, are some of the earliest examples of Renaissance *trompe l'oeil*, also by Peruzzi.

Open: Monday to Saturday 09.00–13.00 hrs. Admission charge.

◆◆◆
VILLA GIULIA
Viale delle Belle Arti
This handsome country house was Julius III's dream villa, its design aided by Giorgio Vasari, better known as an art historian, although the major part of what you see today was the work of Ammannati and Vignola. Julius, the last of the Renaissance popes, spent a fortune on his villa, filling it with classical statuary, much of which was removed to the

WHAT TO SEE

Superb Carracci frescos in the Palazzo Farnese

Vatican after his death.
Today, the villa is a museum, founded in 1889 to house pre-Roman antiques excavated in the provinces of Etruria, Lazio and Umbria. It is the finest of all museums devoted to the Etruscans (a civilisation which so influenced the Romans) and is beautifully laid out in the main block and in the two wings added in this century. Most of the exhibits came from ancient tombs for the Etruscans, who like the Egyptians surrounded their dead with everything they thought they might require in the after life. The *Apollo* and *Hercules* terracotta sculptures are superb as is the sarcophagus of the *Bride and Bridegroom* from Cerveteri, a delicate and touching funerary representation.
The Etruscans traded considerably, as can be seen from the number of Greek

vases and Egyptian scent bottles which have been dug up in Etruria, but they also produced their own pottery, known as *bucchero*, a distinctive black ware frequently decorated with reliefs. Many of the treasures were found in two 7th-century BC tombs at Praeneste, along with cups and dishes in precious metals, leading us to believe that Praeneste was a trend-setting city in its day, a Paris of the ancient world.
Open: 09.00–19.00 hrs Tuesday to Saturday; Sunday to 13.00 hrs (closed Monday). Admission charge.

◆
VILLA MEDICI
Viale Trinità dei Monti
Designed by Annibale Lippi for Cardinal Ricci in 1544, its austere façade has changed little since. In 1580 it was purchased by Cardinal Ferdinando de Medici and after Napoleon grabbed it in 1803, it has housed the French Academy in Rome.

Churches

There are several hundred places of worship in Rome including basilicas (see above) and chapels, each one unique in its own way. Among the most interesting churches are:

◆
S AGNESE IN AGONE
Piazza Navona
Emperor Domitian's stadium once stood on this site, the kind of establishment that would have attracted others of ill repute to set up in the vicinity, which is probably how 13-year-old St Agnese began her martyrdom by being stripped of her clothes in a brothel by the circus. A miraculous growth of hair forthwith covered her nakedness – a scene depicted in marble relief in the church's crypt.

◆
S AGOSTINO
Piazza S Agostino
This church is dedicated to St Augustine, author of *Confessions*, and was in its day the favoured place of worship for Rome's intellectuals. It was built at the end of the 15th century. Note Caravaggio's *Madonna of Loreto* (17th century) in one of the chapels.

◆
S ANDREA DELLA VALLE
Corso Vittorio Emanuele
Best known as the setting for the first act in *Tosca*, this richly decorated baroque church has the city's second highest dome. Of interest inside are two sculpted tombs of the Piccolomini popes, brought from St Peter's in 1614; and the Barberini and Lancellotti family chapels.

◆
S BARTOLOMEO
Piazza S Bartolomeo, Tiber Island
Emperor Otto III built the original church here at the end of the 10th century on the site of the Temple of Aesculapius and it became S Bartolomeo when the saint's relics were transferred here. The most interesting feature is the 12th-century marble wellhead in front of the main altar, probably the site of Aesculapius's (god of healing) spring.

◆
S CARLO ALLE QUATTRO FONTANE
Via del Quirinale
This lovely little oval church, familiarly known as San Carlino, was designed by Borromini in 1634. He masterfully overcame the restrictions of an awkwardly shaped site by clever geometric calculation.

◆
S CECILIA IN TRASTEVERE
Piazza di S Cecilia
What you see today is an 18th-century façade, the work of Ferdinando Fuga, with a medieval portico and a 12th-century campanile. Maderno's statue of Santa Cecilia lies below the high altar, and in the convent beside the church is a Pietro Cavallini masterpiece – a portion of his *Last Judgment* fresco from around 1293. The large marble vase is an original Roman piece.

CENTRAL ROME-CHURCHES

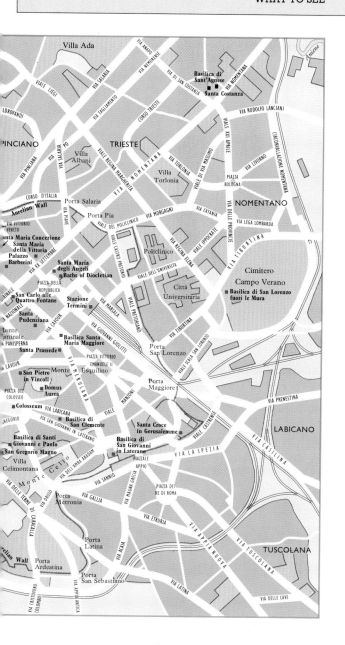

An original Roman marble vase before the 18th-century portico and 12th-century campanile of S Cecilia in Trastevere

◆
SS COSMA E DAMIANO
Via dei Fori Imperiali
Although the Temple of Romulus serves as a vestibule, this church cannot be entered via the Roman Forum, but instead through the cloisters of the adjoining convent. Look at the apse and you will see a golden-robed Christ between St Peter and St Paul, along with the martyred doctors and other saints – brilliant 6th-century craftsmanship.

◆
S COSTANZA
Via di S Agnese, off Via Nomentana
In the 4th century this peaceful site was the mausoleum for Emperor Constantine's daughters, Constantia and Helen. Although located in the suburbs, it is worth the journey to see the exquisite mosaics adorning the vaulting. The designs are ornamental, and are composed of geometric or floral patterns and decorated with cupids, birds and sprays of fruit.

◆
S CROCE IN GERUSALEMME
Piazza S Croce in Gerusalemme
This church's other title is Basilica Sessoriana and it was said to have been built to house the relics of the Cross brought to Rome from Jerusalem, although the present building is of a much later period. The late 15th-century fresco in the apse is attributed to Antonioazzo Romano and shows St Helena's finding of the True Cross.

◆
S FRANCESCA ROMANA
east end of the Roman Forum
The baroque interior of this church glitters with gold and coloured marble, and one of its highlights is the 5th-century encaustic picture of Virgin and Child in the sacristy. In the crypt beneath the confessio (probably designed by Bernini) is the preserved body of S Francesca Romana, who was canonised nearly 400 years ago, in 1608.

◆
S GIORGIO IN VELABRO
Via del Velabro, off Via S Teodoro
The name is derived from the Velabrum or river swamp where legend says Romulus and Remus were found and suckled by the she-wolf, and thanks to skilful renovation in the 1920s, the interior's early origins have been revealed in its antique columns, 13th-century stone altar and canopy and weathered wood ceiling.

◆
S GREGORIO MAGNO
Via di S Gregorio
This is an important Roman church for the British, for according to legend it was from the monastery here that Gregory the Great dispatched St Augustine to England to begin Britain's conversion to Christianity. Some early tombs in the forecourt include that of Sir Edward Carne, an English religious exile. In St Gregory's Chapel a 15th-century altar depicts scenes from his life.

◆
S IGNAZIO
Via S Ignazio
Built to honour the founder of the Jesuit order, Ignatius Loyola, between 1626 and 1685, this church has a magnificent interior including a *trompe l'oeil* ceiling which represents the entry of St Ignatius into Paradise, best viewed from the small disc half way up the nave.

◆
S IVO ALLA SAPIENZA
Corso del Rinascimento, with entrance from the courtyard of Palazzo della Sapienza, No 40.
Another Borromini masterpiece, this is not a church of grand scale, but of imaginative design with a hexagonal ground plan and a fanciful dome topped by a gilded spiral.

◆
S LUIGI DEI FRANCESI
Piazza di S Luigi dei Francesi
This is the French national church in Rome, built during the 16th century. Its greatest treasure is Caravaggio's early work in the Chapel of St Matthew (last on the left), comprising three enormous pictures: the *Calling of St Matthew*, the *Martyrdom of St Matthew* and *St Matthew and the Angel*.

◆
S MARIA DELLA CONCEZIONE
Via Vittorio Veneto
A delightful Cappuccini church with a macabre array of thousands of old bones covering vaults and walls and, in some niches, entire skeletons in cowled robes.

◆
S MARIA IN COSMEDIN
Piazza Bocca della Verità
Outside in the portico here is the Bocca della Verità or 'mouth of truth', a large round stone used by the ancient Romans as a drain cover. During the Middle Ages the legend was created that anyone who held his hand in this stone's gaping mouth and told a lie, would lose his fingers – a challenge few can resist even today!

WHAT TO SEE

♦♦
S MARIA SOPRA MINERVA
Piazza della Minerva
Rome's only Gothic church, this one was built within the ruins of the Temple of Minerva in 1280, and is noted for Filippino Lippi's marvellous frescos (painted about 1489). Another treasure is Michelangelo's *Christ bearing the Cross* (on the left hand side of the high altar), executed between 1514 and 1521 though the gilded drapery and sandal were added later – the latter to protect the foot from being worn away by the faithful's kisses.

The convent adjoining the church was the scene of Galileo Galilei's famous trial when he was condemned by the Inquisition for insisting that the earth moves around the sun and not vice versa.

♦
S MARIA DELLA PACE
Vicolo della Pace
This tiny church, designed by Baccio Pontelli around 1480, was built as a result of Sixtus IV's vow when war against the Florentines stopped.
According to legend, the picture of the Virgin now hanging over the altar, bled when pierced by a sword, causing Sixtus IV to come in state to view the miraculous picture and promise to dedicate a church to the Virgin if she would bring the hostilities to an end. Don't miss Raphael's fresco of the Sibyls, in the first chapel on the right, or the superb cloisters designed by Bramante in 1502.

♦
S MARIA DEL POPOLO
Piazza del Popolo
In the first chapel of the left transept here are splendid paintings by Michelangelo Caravaggio (1601–2), depicting the *Conversion of St Paul* and the *Crucifixion of St Peter* and also of note is the octagonal Chigi Chapel, designed by Raphael for a wealthy Roman banker.

♦
S MARIA IN TRASTEVERE
Piazza di S Maria in Trastevere
This was the first of Rome's churches to be dedicated to the Virgin and may well be the city's oldest though much of what we see today is due to Innocent II's rebuilding in the 12th century. The mosaics inside the church are exceptional.

♦
S MARIA DELLA VITTORIA
Via XX Settembre ·
The showpiece of this excellent example of fine baroque decor is Bernini's Coronaro Chapel in the left transept, built between 1645 and 1652, showing members of the Coronaro family in such a way they appear to be in theatre boxes watching the centrepiece scene, the *Ecstasy of St Teresa*.

♦
S PIETRO IN MONTORIO
Via Garibaldi
Although this church is said to have been built on the site where St Peter was crucified, the claim is actually rather doubtful. It is most celebrated

Part of the sumptuous interior of S Maria in Trastevere

for Bramante's *Tempietto*, or little temple, just outside in the courtyard, erected in 1502, where in the crypt you can see a hole said to be where St Peter's cross stood.

◆◆
S PIETRO IN VINCOLI
Piazza di S Pietro in Vincoli
This church was built by Sixtus III in 432 to house the chains said to have bound St Peter when he was captive in Jerusalem, and later the chains said to have bound him in Rome were added. According to legend, the two sets of chains were miraculously joined together, and are now kept in a bronze and crystal casket in the confessional beneath the high altar. Make sure you also see the statue of Moses by Michelangelo.

◆
S PRASSEDE
Via S Prassede, off Piazza di S Maria Maggiore
This church was built in the 9th century by St Paschal I. It is best known for its mosaics, especially in the nave and in the Chapel of Zenone, built by Paschal as a mausoleum for his mother. Black granite columns mark its entrance, while the walls and vaulted ceiling are encrusted with gold mosaics portraying Christ and the Apostles, the Madonna and Child, and St Prassede and her sister St Pudenziana.

◆
S PUDENZIANA
Via Urbana
Traditionally believed to have been built on the site of the house where St Peter lived for seven years, archaeologists have found that the building had in fact formed part of 2nd century Roman baths. The *pièce de résistance* is the 5th-century apse mosaic, showing a golden-robed Christ with his apostles and SS Prassede and Pudenziana. Remains of the baths can still be seen today, behind the apse.

◆◆
S SABINA
Piazza di S Pietro d'Illiria
This is a supreme example of a 5th-century basilica, and the greatest prizes are the carved cypress panels of the west doors. Eighteen of the 5th-century originals still survive, making them among the oldest wooden works of art in existence.

Museums

◆◆◆
DOMUS AUREA (NERO'S GOLDEN HOUSE)

Via Labicana 136

Nero may or may not have 'fiddled while Rome burned' as the legend would have it, but he certainly built himself a fantasy palace covered with gold and furnished to the utmost luxury of his time. There were indoor baths, fed by the sea and sulphur springs with hot and cold running water, beautiful murals executed by some of the day's leading artists, and coffered ivory ceilings.

You will need a little imagination, visiting Domus Aurea today, to appreciate how exotic and light and airy it would have been then, sitting on a high terrace, compared to how dank and gloomy it seems now. But that is because Trajan built his public baths over the Golden House when it was destroyed by fire in 104.

The magnificent handiwork of the original architects, Severus and Celeres, is now lost for ever, but come with a powerful torch and opera glasses to aid you, and the faded paintings will become much more visible.

The most famous rooms are grouped around the domed octagonal hall of the dining room where once sumptuous banquets were given at a revolving table, and the Sala della Volta (the room with the gilded vault) or entrance hall. *Open:* daily 09.00–13.00 hrs (closed Monday). Admission charge.

◆
MUSEO DELLE ARTI E TRADIZIONI POPOLARI

Piazza Marconi 8

Just outside central Rome at the EUR, this museum houses a vast collection of everything concerning Italian life at the turn of the century. *Open:* daily 09.00–14.00 hrs; Sunday to 13.00 hrs (closed Monday).

◆
MUSEO CENTRALE DEL RISORGIMENTO

Via S Pietro in Carcere

This museum next to the Monument to Victor Emmanuel contains an abundance of historical archive material from the Napoleonic occupation to the unification of Italy. *Open:* Wednesday, Friday, Sunday 10.00–13.00 hrs.

◆
MUSEO DEL FOLKLORE

Piazza S'Egidio

Scenes from Roman 18th- and 19th-century daily life are represented by dioramas in this Trastevere museum; the collection of paintings, drawings and early photographs is gradually being expanded. *Open:* daily 09.00–13.00 hrs; Thursday also 17.00–19.30 hrs (closed Monday). Admission charge.

◆
MUSEO PREISTORICO ED ETNOGRAFICO LUIGI PIGNORINI

Viale Lincoln 1

Another museum in the EUR, this houses a comprehensive

Palazzo Barberini, home of the Galleria Nazionale d'Arte Antica

collection of items that chart the development and ethnography of the prehistoric ages with particular reference to Italy.
Open: 09.00–14.00 hrs, Tuesday, Friday, Saturday to 18.00 hrs; Sunday 09.00–13.00 hrs (closed Monday). Admission charge.

◆◆◆
PALAZZO BARBERINI (BARBERINI PALACE)
Via delle Quattro Fontane
This splendid baroque palace, begun by Carlo Maderno in 1625 and completed by Bernini in 1633, is the home of one of Rome's finest museums, the **Galleria Nazionale d'Arte Antica** (National Gallery of Early Art). In actual fact, the word 'antica' is a little misleading.

This palace just contains the 'earlier' part of the National collection. Among the highlights on view here are: a 15th-century Fra Angelico triptych showing the *Ascension, Pentecost and Last Judgment*, two Filippo Lippi works and Lorenzo Lotto's *Portrait of a Young Man*. If you come to see only one picture it must be Raphael's *Fornarina*, the baker's daughter. The model is said to have been his mistress. Also superb are two striking El Grecos, *Adoration of the Shepherds* and *Baptism of Christ* as well as Tintoretto's *Christ and the Woman taken in Adultery*. Notable in the rooms displaying works by Flemish and German artists is Quentin Massy's *Erasmus* and Holbein's *Henry VIII*.
Open: daily 09.00–14.00 hrs; Sunday to 13.00 hrs (closed Monday). Admission charge.

WHAT TO SEE

The Borghese Gallery – housed in the Casino of the Villa Borghese

in the casino of the Villa Borghese (see Villa Borghese). It was founded by Paul V's nephew, Cardinal Scipione Borghese, Bernini's first patron, and the collection remained housed in the palace until 1891.

Although the palace is not open to the public, its courtyard and garden are worth a look. One of its most colourful inhabitants was Pauline Bonaparte, Napoleon's favourite sister, who married Camillo Borghese in 1803 and due to her curious ways, became a legend in her own time.

Open: daily 09.00–14.00 hrs; Tuesday and Thursday also 17.00–20.00 hrs; Sunday 09.00–13.00 hrs (closed Monday). Admission charge.

◆

PALAZZO BORGHESE (BORGHESE PALACE)

Largo della Fontanella Borghese

Owing to its curious shape, this sumptuous palace is often referred to as *il cembalo* (the harpsichord) whose graceful portal by Flaminio Ponzio suggests the keyboard. When Cardinal Borghese became Paul V in 1605, he bought the 16th-century palace for a family home and it has remained in that family's hands ever since.

The Borghese's love of the arts was the basis for the superb collection now known as the Borghese Gallery and housed

◆◆

PALAZZO BRASCHI (BRASCHI PALACE)

Piazza S Pantaleo 10

This palace, built in 1780 for Pius VI's nephew, was the last one to be erected in Rome for the family of a pope. Today it houses the **Rome Museum**, devoted to all aspects of the city's life from the Middle Ages onwards. Students and specialists will find the print room on the top floor of great interest and benefit to research, but the museum also houses general curiosities including Pius IX's personal railway carriage.

Open: daily 09.00–14.00 hrs; Tuesday and Thursday also 17.00–20.00 hrs; Sunday 09.00–13.00 hrs (closed Monday). Admission charge.

◆
PALAZZO COLONNA
(COLONNA PALACE)

*Piazza Santi Apostoli –
entrance in Via della Pilotta*
Colonna Pope Martin V
founded this palace in the 15th
century, though the bulk of
what you see today dates from
1730, when it was rebuilt. It
houses the **Colonna Gallery**, a
private collection of paintings
which include some historic
family portraits, among them
Michelangelo's friend, Vittorio
Colonna, and Louis XIV's first
love, Marie Mancini. More
important artistically, however,
are the Gaspard Dughet
landscapes, Tintoretto's
Narcissus and Annibale
Carracci's *Bean Eater*.
Open: Saturday 09.00–13.00
hrs (closed August). Admission
charge.

◆◆
PALAZZO CORSINI
(CORSINI PALACE)

Via della Lungara
Built in the 15th century for
Cardinal Domenico Riario, the
Palazzo Corsini became Queen
Christina of Sweden's
residence in the 17th century
when she gave up her throne
for the Catholic faith.
The elegant façade you see
today was added by
Ferdinando Fuga a century
later. The upper floors now
house the later part of the
**Galleria Nazional d'Arte
Antica**. Among the most
notable works are two
Caravaggios: *Narcissus* and *St
John the Baptist*, Rubens' *St
Sebastian*, and Van Dyck's

*Paolina Borghese, Napoleon
Bonaparte's sister, by Canova*

Rest on the Flight to Egypt.
Open: 09.00–14.00 hrs (closed
Monday). Admission charge.

♦♦♦
PALAZZO DORIA
(DORIA PALACE)
Piazza del Collegio Romano
The façade presented today is
18th-century, by Gabriele
Valvassori (overlooking the
Corso) and by Paolo Ameli (on
the Via del Plebiscito) and
17th-century by Antonio del
Grande (on the Piazza del
Collegio Romano). The palace,
built in the 15th century for
Cardinal Fazio Santorio is a
mixture of many styles and
periods and has passed
through many a noble family's
hands including the
Aldobrandini, the Pamphilj and
the Dorias. It is famous for the
Galleria Doria Pamphilj whose
greatest treasure is the
Velasquez portrait of the
Pamphilj pope, Innocent X.
The collection is one of Rome's
most important in a setting of
equal magnificence. Among
the most outstanding pictures
are two Titians, *Religion
Succoured by Spain* and
Salome; three Caravaggios, *St
Mary Magdalen, Rest on the
Flight into Egypt* and *St John
the Baptist*; and Raphael's
Double Portrait, all in the first
gallery. Of the state
apartments, the Yellow Salon is
particularly charming with its
twelve exquisite Gobelin
tapestries made for Louis XV.
The private apartments are still
lived in and contain many fine
family mementoes in the
Andrea Doria Room and a
Sebastiano del Piombo portrait

The splendours of Palazzo Doria

of that famous admiral in the
large green drawing room.
Open: Tuesday, Friday,
Saturday, Sunday 10.00–13.00
hrs. Admission charge.

♦
PALAZZO FARNESE
(FARNESE PALACE)
Piazza Farnese
Rome's first Renaissance
palace is the French Embassy
and no longer open to the
public.
It is the combined work of
Antonio Sangallo the Younger,
Michelangelo and Giacomo
della Porta, and was
completed finally in 1589.

PALAZZO MADAMA (MADAMA PALACE)

Corso del Rinascimento

A 16th-century palace with a 17th-century façade by Paolo Maruscelli, nowadays the seat of the upper house of the Italian parliament, it takes its name from Margaret of Austria, Emperor Charles V's illegitimate daughter.

PALAZZO MASSIMO ALLE COLONNE (PALACE OF MASSIMO COLONNE)

Corso Vittorio Emanuele

After the sack of Rome in 1527, this Baldassare Peruzzi masterpiece was designed for the Massimo family, taking its name from the great columns which were a feature of its predecessor. Architecturally, it is unique with its curved façade and ingenious use of its narrow and difficult site. It is not open to the public but you may just glimpse the vestibule's stuccoed ceiling and the courtyard beyond.

PALAZZO DEL QUIRINALE (THE QUIRINAL PALACE)

Piazza del Quirinale

The official residence of the Italian president these days was once a papal address. When the Vatican decided it needed a better location for a

WHAT TO SEE

summer residence they chose the site where previously Cardinal Ippolito d'Este, illegitimate son of Alfonso d'Este and Lucrezia Borgia, had his town palace and gardens on one of the seven original hills of Rome. Quirinale was begun in 1574 by Martino Longhi, whose work was carried on by a distinguished list of architects including Carlo Maderno, Bernini and Fuga. It remained a papal residence until 1870. Tours take about an hour and one of the main sights is the fragment of Melozzo da Forli's *Last Judgment*, formerly in the church of SS Apostoli and one of the most striking salons is the Hall of Mirrors with its Murano glass chandeliers.
Open: by appointment only through written application.

◆
PALAZZO SPADA (SPADA PALACE)
Piazza Capodiferro
This decoratively stuccoed 16th-century palace became the property of Cardinal Bernardino Spada in 1632 and stayed in family hands until it was sold to the State in 1926. The overloaded stuccoed façade is the work of Giulio Mazzoni, but the most celebrated feature is the *trompe l'oeil* perspective in the garden gallery, added by Borromini and giving the appearance of a long colonnade ending in a courtyard adorned by a large statue. The optical illusion is impressive for in fact the colonnade is short and the

statue tiny. When the state rooms are not being used by the Council of State, they may be visited, but the main reason for coming here is the **Galleria Spada**, a small but worthy private collection of art started by Cardinal Spada and added to by subsequent generations, including Titian's unfinished *Portrait of a Musician* and Andrea del Sarto's *Visitation*. The best pictures in the third rooms are Jan Breughel's *Landscape with Windmills* and Rubens' *A Cardinal*.
Open: daily 09.00–14.00 hrs; Sunday to 13.00 hrs (closed Monday). Admission charge.

◆
PALAZZO VENEZIA (PALACE OF VENICE)
Via del Plebiscito
Venetian Pope Paul II built this first great Renaissance palace of Rome in 1455. He was an avid collector of art and filled his home with many *objets d'art*, silver and gold wares, tapestries and brocades. It seems only appropriate therefore that the **Palazzo Venezia Museum** as it is today should be chiefly devoted to the arts and crafts of medieval and Renaissance times. There is much fine sculpture, including a pope by Arnolfo di Cambio and handsome Barsanti bronzes.
The papal apartment, whose Sala del Mappamondo was used by Mussolini as his office, has been completely restored to its original style.
Open: 09.00–14.00 hrs; Sunday to 13.00 hrs (closed Monday). Admission charge.

Excursions from Rome

◆
CASTEL GANDOLFO

Lazio 15 miles (25 km)

The Pope's summer residence overlooks scenic Lake Albano among the delightful rolling hills of Colli Albani. The original palace was built by Urban VIII in 1624 and has been used by most pontiffs since. The villa's park is not open to the public but contains the Vatican's Observatory telescopes.

According to popular legend, Castel Gandolfo was built over the ruins of Alba Longa, founded by Ascanius as a chief town in the days of the kings of Rome, though these days it shows little trace of that glorious era.

◆
CERVETERI

Lazio 28 miles (46 km)

Once known as Caere, this was a wealthy and powerful Etruscan city. Although remains are few, the necropolis area when excavated yielded many of the treasures to be seen in the Villa Giulia in Rome. The tomb area, built with paved streets between the rows of *tumuli*, is located just about a mile from the village. The tombs date back to the 6th century BC, some still showing remnants of their original paintings and reliefs, and many constructed as replicas of Etruscan houses. A tour of the area known as Necropolis della Banditaccia will probably take two hours

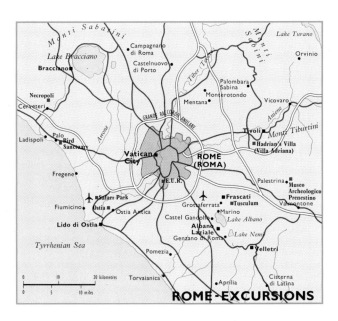

ROME-EXCURSIONS

and special permission may be needed (from the Villa Giulia) to see one of the most fascinating – the Tomb of the Reliefs.

◆◆
FRASCATI
Lazio 14 miles (22 km)
In addition to the fine wines produced here, this sizeable town is notable also for its country estates. It is, therefore, a perfect destination for a day's outing into the Roman countryside to visit the Castelli Romani. You may certainly visit Villa Torlonia (now a public park) and the Villa Aldobrandini, which was built for Pope Clement VII's nephew, Cardinal Aldobrandini, in 1598. The view from its terraces is incredible. The town's main square is the Piazza Marconi and the ruined Roman town of Tusculum, where Cicero once had a villa, are worth a brief visit.

◆
GENZANO
Lazio 19 miles (30 km)
Starting point for a visit to Lake Nemi which was known as 'Diana's Mirror' in olden times. At the lakeside, a small museum houses the remains of two large Roman ships built in AD 37 during Caligula's reign and used for festivals on the lake.
On the wooded slopes that reach down to the lake, wild strawberries grow in abundance in spring and these 'fragolini' are as popular with visitors and locals today as they were in the time of Nero.

◆
GROTTAFERRATA
Lazio 13 miles (23 km)
A peaceful place most famous for its abbey, founded in 1004 and a centre of Greek scholarship. One of the monks will show you around the monastery, which has a library of rare Greek manuscripts and a museum of religious treasures. Before he became Pope Julius II, Guiliano della Rovere was abbot here. The Church of Santa Maria has a splendid 12th-century campanile and the frescos in the Chapel of San Nilo are by Domenichino.

◆◆
LAKE BRACCIANO
Lazio 24 miles (39 km)
The lake fills a volcanic crater in the Sabatini hills northwest of Rome and is bordered by a number of sailing clubs and waterside *trattorie* specialising in fish caught in its waters. Its pine and olive planted shores are pleasant for picnics and swimming.
The town of Bracciano itself, overlooking the lake, is worth visiting to see the Castello Orsini, a fine example of a private Renaissance castle built around 1485 for the Orsini family. A number of the rooms still contain their original frescos and an assortment of family heirlooms are also displayed.

◆◆◆
OSTIA ANTICA
Lazio 17 miles (28 km)
Rome's ancient seaport, Ostia is one of the most interesting excursions you can make. Its

Ruins of an ancient seaport at nearby Ostia Antica

ruins offer insight into daily urban life up to the 2nd century when its prosperity began to decline. Barbaric invasions and a malaria epidemic finally killed the place but the sand which covered the ruins has preserved much for us to see today.

On the main street, *Decumanus Maximus*, you can see paving stones rutted by chariot wheels. As at Pompeii, many of the houses show their original mosaic or inlaid marble floors and the old Roman equivalent of a bar, the *Thermopolium*, has a marble drinks counter. Some of the more interesting items uncovered by excavation are displayed in the small museum (though opening times are somewhat variable). In summer, open air performances are given in the old theatre.

◆
PALESTRINA
Lazio 24 miles (38 km)
In prehistoric times this was Praeneste, already a thriving community in the 7th century BC for the Etruscans. A Temple of Fortune existed here from the 6th century BC, a vast religious complex that was reconstructed by the Romans in the 2nd century BC on six terraced levels on the hillside. Amidst its ruins, the Colonna family built a palace which now houses the **Museo Archeologico Prenestino** (or Archaeological Museum), best known for a marvellous mosaic of the River Nile. This mosaic once decorated the floor of the Sala Absidata, now just an assortment of stones and columns which flanks the heart of the town, Piazza Regina Margherita.

WHAT TO SEE

◆◆◆
TIVOLI
Lazio 19 miles (31 km)

Undoubtedly the most popular excursion from Rome in order to see Hadrian's Villa, now in ruins, and the Villa d'Este, renowned for its gardens. Many a wealthy Roman built a summer villa here. Hadrian's was the most splendid, built in the 2nd century to recreate those places which had most impressed him. He loved the Poikile, the massive colonnaded entrance which came from Athens, and he imitated the canal and temple to Serapis he had seen in Egypt. He died shortly after the completion of his sumptuous retreat and over the centuries the amazing marble work and statuary has been plundered, but this place is still evocative.

Cardinal Ippolito d'Este was one who did not hesitate to use the old Hadrian estate as a quarry for his own villa, constructed in 1550. His water gardens with their 500 fountains are probably as famous now as when he created them, though the Organ Fountain no longer produces music, nor the Owl Fountain the sounds of birdsong. It is still worth seeing for the ornamental pools and tall jets of water.

Gardens of the Villa d'Este in the Lazio hills at Tivoli

PEACE AND QUIET

Wildlife and Countryside in and around Rome
by Paul Sterry

When in Rome many visitors choose not to adopt the lifestyle of the city dwellers but rather opt to spend at least part of their time in the surrounding countryside. Rural, agricultural land, scrub-covered hillsides and historic sites lie only a short distance from the city and are full of natural history interest. With a little more effort and with a car, several parks, reserves and wildlife refuges are also within a day's journey of Rome. A trip inland will take you to Abruzzo National Park with its superb, mountainous scenery and alpine plants and animals. By contrast, a journey along the coast reaches either Circeo National Park to the south or three interesting wildlife centres to the north, all of which retain many of the elements of unspoilt Italy.

Circeo National Park

Circeo National Park protects a beautiful stretch of Italian coast less than 60 miles (100 km) south of Rome. Its park status has helped buffer it from development, but it is still affected by considerable pressure from visitors. However, despite its popularity, Circeo's lakes, ponds, beaches, forests and Mediterranean scrub remain rich in wildlife, and quiet spots can always be found by walking the park's trails and paths or by visiting the island of Zannone. In addition to its

Green hairstreak, one of the region's many colourful insects

natural history, Circeo has rich archaeological interest, including prehistoric and Roman remains.

The beaches and dunes here have been colonised by maritime plants such as sea knotgrass, rock samphire and cottonweed, while away from the sea, more established areas of land support typical Mediterranean *maquis* vegetation: aromatic plants of thyme, rosemary and juniper, together with cistuses, broom and dwarf fan palms. The flowers attract insects such as hummingbird hawk moths, chafer beetles and butterflies, including green hairstreak, long-tailed blue and cleopatra. On broken and stony ground, green lizards and wall lizards will probably be seen during the summer months.

The lakes and marshes along the coast are attractive to birds throughout the year. In spring and summer they are favoured

PEACE AND QUIET

Black-winged stilts wade in deep water in search of invertebrates

by collared pratincoles, little egrets, black-winged stilts, avocets, spoonbills and migrant waders such as ruff, wood sandpipers and marsh sandpipers. Terns and gulls of several species are occasional visitors and, in winter, there are often large numbers of wildfowl and coots.

Circeo's forests of holm oak, cork oak, Turkey oak, ash and maple are home to mammals such as wild boar, roe deer, pine marten, beech marten and the introduced Indian mongoose. Golden orioles serenade visitors with their fluty song in spring, and great spotted woodpeckers search trunks and branches for insects. Where dense *maquis* vegetation grows under the cover of woodland, Sardinian warblers, subalpine warblers, woodchat shrikes and serins can be found. Strawberry trees and heathers flourish in sunny clearings, as do such exciting plants as tongue orchids, woodcock orchids and brown bee orchids.

Abruzzo National Park

The Apenine Mountains dominate the middle of Italy and form a backbone to the country. While much of the landscape and wildlife of this rugged central region has been altered or reduced over the centuries, the land which comprises Abruzzo National Park has remained more or less unspoilt. Dramatic mountains, forests of beech and pine, colourful alpine meadows, rushing torrents and limestone *karst* with potholes and caves make this one of the most exciting destinations in central Italy. At just over 98 miles (150 km) from Rome, Abruzzo can be visited in a day, but in order to get the most of the park, at least one night's stay is worthwhile. Above the treeline, alpine meadows and scree slopes are a colourful sight in spring and summer with bearberry, bilberry, alpine snowbells, gentians and saxifrages in profusion. Despite the altitude, a few species of butterfly survive here, and these upland zones are also home to Alpine choughs, rock partridges, rock thrushes, Alpine accentors, water pipits and snow finches. The comparatively lush alpine grazing ensures the survival of good numbers of chamois. These delightful creatures are extremely sure-footed on the uneven terrain and are sometimes obligingly confiding. Young or sick chamois occasionally fall victim to golden eagles or to the park's few remaining wolves. The wolves, like the chamois themselves, belong to an Apennine sub-species which is distinct from other European populations.

The wooded slopes of Abruzzo comprise large areas of beech as well as ash, holly and maple. The leaf canopy is generally dense, but in glades and clearings, stinking hellebores and orchids including military orchid and lady's slipper orchid can be found. The forests also harbour small numbers of European brown bears as well as red deer, roe deer, wild cats and beech martens. Great-spotted and middle-spotted woodpeckers are found in the forests, but a careful look at each bird might just reveal it to be one of the park's white-backed woodpeckers, a decidedly scarce and local bird in Europe.

Orbetello and Mount Argentario

Orbetello Nature Reserve, managed by the World Wide Fund for Nature, protects part of the sand tombolo and tidal lagoons that connect Mount Argentario to mainland Italy. Access to the reserve itself is limited to certain times of the day and week, so either take a chance or check in advance with the WWF. However, much of the surrounding land, which comprises dunes, marshes, fields and woodlands, can be viewed from roads and paths. The reserve is 112 miles (162 km) northwest of Rome.

Spring sees the arrival of migrant birds, many of which are merely passing by, but some of which stay on to nest. Regular nesting migrants include black-winged stilts, bee-eaters, hoopoes, great

A great-spotted woodpecker

PEACE AND QUIET

spotted cuckoos and Montagu's harriers, which supplement numbers of resident Kentish plovers, stone curlews and Sardinian warblers. The variety and numbers of migrant waterbirds is often astonishing, with species including garganey, wood sandpipers, marsh sandpipers, avocets, little egrets and several species of tern. In winter, great white egrets appear along with large numbers of wildfowl, including pintail, teal, shelduck and greylag goose.

Maremma

A short drive to the north of Orbetello Nature Reserve lies Maremma Regional Park near the town of Grosetto. It is a haven which has so far escaped the development that has changed much of Italy's coastline. Access is allowed only at weekends and public

Wild boar are found in woodland

holidays, and because visitor numbers are strictly limited, the peace and quiet of the area is maintained.

Along the coast, the sand dunes can be explored in the hope of finding unusual maritime plants, or perhaps birds such as Kentish plovers. Marshes and drainage ditches are home to fish, and to amphibians such as edible frogs and tree frogs, which fall victim to grass snakes, egrets and herons.

Away from the influence of the sea, Mediterranean *maquis* vegetation develops, with holm oak, cork oak and stone pines growing with an understorey of tree heathers, cistuses, brooms and strawberry trees. Sawfly orchids, woodcock orchids and tongue orchids grow in early spring, which is when eyed lizards and wall lizards are most easily seen. Wild boar, fallow deer, pine martens, serins, wrynecks, hoopoes and short-toed eagles may also be found by more persistent searching.

Lago di Burano Wildlife Refuge

Lago di Burano lies to the south of Orbetello and Maremma and was established as a reserve by the World Wide Fund for Nature in 1967 in order to protect migrating and wintering water birds. A brackish lake is the main attraction of the refuge, but its fringes of reedbeds and the surrounding *maquis* vegetation are also rich in wildlife. Public access is restricted to two days a week unless a prior arrangement has been made, but a visit is well worthwhile and is enhanced by the presence of a hide and a nature trail.

Among the exciting birds that visit the reserve in winter are tufted ducks, wigeon, pochards, ferruginous ducks, red-crested pochards, grebes and the occasional flamingo and spoonbill. In spring, Montagu's harriers, Baillon's crakes, great reed warblers and Cetti's warblers grace the reedbeds. The adjacent woodland and *maquis* has many colourful flowers in the spring. Bee-eaters hunt for insects overhead, making their characteristic liquid calls, while Sardinian and subalpine warblers sing from the cover of bushes and shrubs.

An aptly named tongue orchid

Bird migration

Large numbers of European birds spend the summer months on their breeding territories and fly south to Africa for the winter. The Mediterranean is a major obstacle in their path and many use the Italian peninsula to reduce flight distances over the sea. The western coast of Italy acts as a natural route for migrants in spring and autumn, with thousands passing through the Roman countryside from March to May and from August to October.

Migrant birds are often grounded by sudden bad weather and then stop off to feed and rest. It is worth remembering that each species is attracted to a preferred habitat, and thus marshes and lakes should be searched for ducks, terns, gulls, waders, pratincoles and white storks, while bee-eaters, warblers, bluethroats and birds of prey will be found in open country. The birds can face a very tough time, since many Italians think it is great fun to shoot and trap them. Everything from blackcap to honey buzzard is at risk, but hopefully a growing environmental awareness in the country will soon put a stop to this senseless slaughter.

Spring flowers

In common with most of the Mediterranean region, the countryside around Rome is hot and dry in summer, and mild and wet in winter. This marked seasonality is reflected in the appearance of the plants, many of which dry

PEACE AND QUIET

A beautiful woodcock orchid

up during the summer months leaving only withered stems, often encrusted with aestivating (summer hibernating) snails. Winter is the season of growth for most wild flowers in lowland Italy, with the majority bursting into flower between February and May.

Olive groves, cultivated fields and open, stony ground are all good searching places for the botanist. Corn marigolds, gladioli, asphodels and thistles all appear in a profusion now unfamiliar to visitors from countries with more intensive agriculture. Such colourful meadows often echo to the repetitive calls of quails. Open areas on well-drained soil might harbour tongue orchids, lizard orchids, yellow bee orchids, woodcock orchids and many others. It is worth looking closely at all sorts of rough-looking areas; these are often the ones where the really exciting finds are made.

Open country

Most of the evergreen woodland which would once have cloaked the Roman countryside has long since disappeared. With the exception of a few parks, reserves and private estates the landscape has been transformed by man. However, in many areas, the attractive form of shrubby vegetation known as *maquis* or *macchia* has developed, often under the shade of scattered trees. Although this is essentially a man-made habitat, created by grazing and by the removal of the original vegetation, it has been around for so long now that many of its plants and animals have become specialised and are found nowhere else.

Strawberry trees, tree heathers, broom and cistuses are characteristic shrubs in these areas, with a ground layer of colourful, and often aromatic, plants such as thyme, rosemary, sage and myrtle. Green, eyed and wall lizards feast on grasshoppers and crickets, and in turn fall victim to Aesculapian snakes and asps. Hermann's tortoises, on the other hand, have an essentially herbivorous diet. It can be a special thrill to catch your first glimpse of one of these lumbering, enchanting creatures. Characteristic birds of open country include Sardinian, subalpine and Dartford warblers, short-toed larks, serins and bee-eaters.

FOOD AND DRINK

Eating Out

You might expect to eat excellent Italian food in Rome and the Romans love their own type of cuisine more than anyone else's. So while there are many other ethnic restaurants in the city, the majority still cook Italian-style – from traditional regional specialities to a local family style.

Rome is itself a capital of a region and its specialities range from those of peasant origin – based on basic ingredients such as chick peas, tripe, salt cod, sweetbreads and pasta – to those more luxurious delicacies like *abbacchio* (baby lamb seasoned with sage, garlic, rosemary and anchovy paste), or *capretto alforno* (roast kid). Other Roman dishes to look out for include: *carciofi alla giudia* (artichokes deep-fried in olive oil and lemon juice, to look like open flowers when cooked); *stracciatella* (a clear soup into which egg, semolina and cheese has been beaten); *saltimbocca alla Romana* (veal escalope covered with sage leaves and ham); and *piselli al proscuitto* (peas slowly cooked with Parma ham and diced bacon).

For the locals, a good meal is preferable to most other kinds of entertainment and is likely to be a long one. They will start off with *antipasto*, a selection of hors d'ouevres, and follow it with a soup *(minestra)*, broth with pasta *(pasta in brodo)* or a *pasta asciutta* (spaghetti, tagliatelle, *etc*) – *spaghetti alla carbonara* (spaghetti with bacon, black pepper, eggs and pecorino cheese) or *spaghetti all'Amatriciana* (spaghetti with fresh tomato sauce, bacon, onion and pecorino), both Roman specialities.

Then comes the main course, usually divided into two on the menu: there are dishes of the day *(piatti del giorno)*, which are usually the best, or dishes which have to be specially made *(piatti da farsi)*. Several very fine Rome restaurants specialise in seafood, but be prepared for an expensive bill if you select fish, whether fresh or frozen. (Restaurants are obliged by law to specify on their menus whether their seafood is straight from the sea or the freezer.)

Romans generally conclude a filling meal with something light; more often than not, fresh fruit or a *macedonia* fruit cup. Fresh cheese is another favourite – *ricotta* perhaps (cottage cheese made from ewe's milk), sprinkled with sugar, or small scoops of *mozzarella*. But most people agree the best dessert to choose in Rome is *gelato* – ice cream; the city is celebrated for it. The finest ice cream is made only with eggs, milk, cream, sugar and fresh fruit and is best sampled in a *gelateria* rather than a restaurant. Ice cream parlours are scattered throughout Rome and since visitors and residents alike have their preferences it is hard to say

FOOD AND DRINK

Italians make great ice cream; Giolitti has some of the best

which is number one. Most discerning Romans agree that the best ice-cream in the city comes from **Bar San Filippo**, tucked away in fashionable Parioli at Via di Villa San Filippo 8, although **Giolitti**, in Via Uffici del Vicario 40, has its devotees. Growing in popularity is the trendy **Gelateria della Palma**, in Via della Maddalena 20, where you can choose from over 100 different flavours: the *semi-freddi* (semi-frozen creams) and *cremolati* (water ices) are to be recommended.

The final touch, *espresso*, is a speciality of some cafés. One of the best *espressos* in the city can be taken at **La Tazza d'Oro**, Via Degli Orfani 84, a bar selling nothing but coffee. The **Sant'Eustachio**, on Piazza Sant'Eustachio 82, froths up a quite marvellous *cappucino*. Remember that in Rome, as elsewhere in Italy, you pay more for a sit-down coffee than one at a stand-up bar. Romans, themselves, prefer *à la carte* menus and certainly the best food is ordered this way, but that is not to say fixed-price menus do not exist – look for the *menu turistico* sign, or the words *prezzo fisso*. In an *à la carte* restaurant you can expect a cover charge and often an additional charge for bread whether or not you eat it. Even when service is included (usually at 15 per cent), a waiter will expect an extra 10 per cent. The fixed price menu usually includes a first and second course, vegetables and dessert, the bread and cover charge and sometimes the house wine. There are literally thousands of eating places in Rome to suit every style and budget. In a luxury establishment, a complete meal for two with a good bottle of wine is likely to cost Lit 140,000 plus. In a highly regarded restaurant, probably family owned, the price guideline is Lit 100,000 for two and in a middle of the road restaurant, Lit 60,000–70,000. If budget is tight, look for the ubiquitous *pizzeria*, snack bars, fast food outlets (there is a McDonald's near the Piazza di Spagna) or any sign that reads *tavole calde* and *tavole fredde* (hot and cold buffets).

Theoretically, *ristorante* is a restaurant in the accepted sense, while a *trattoria* is a more simple eating place and the *osteria or hostaria*, more simple still. In practice, this is not necessarily so, the **Hostaria dell'Orso**, for example, is famous and fancy.

Because eating out is such a pastime, there is no one defined area of Rome for good restaurants. A recommended district, however, is Trastevere (also the oldest) where most of the countless dining spots have outdoor tables for summer use. Eating *al fresco* any time between April and October is very much the Roman custom.

Roman Specialities

The Romans are so in love with their own cuisine that there are literally countless restaurants offering speciality dishes. Among the best in the Trastevere area are: **Comparone**, Piazza in Piscinula 47 (tel: 581 6249) which serves traditional dishes of brains, sweetbreads, liver and tripe, plus grills for the less adventurous. **Sabatini**, Piazza Santa Maria in Trastevere 13 (tel: 582 026) is another famous name when it comes to authentic cooking and fish. This is a popular eating place, but if you cannot get in, or it is a Wednesday when the restaurant closes, try the newer branch, **Sabatini-II** at Vicolo Santa Maria in Trastevere (tel: 588 307), which is closed on Tuesdays instead. **Romolo**, Via Porta Settimiana 8 (tel: 588 284), offers a wide range of meat and pasta dishes in historical surroundings; in summer, most prefer to eat in its enchanting courtyard, bounded by the Aurelian Wall. Also recommended in this area are the **Taverna Trilussa**, Via del Politeama (tel: 581 8918) whose dishes include pasta with sausages; **Checco er Carettiere**, Via Benedetta 14 (tel: 581 7018) for a wide choice that includes fish and **Meo Patacca**, Piazza de Mercanti 30 (tel: 581 6198) has music and folklore.

Near the Colosseum, **Taverna dei Quaranta**, Via Claudia 24 (tel: 736 296) offers some of the best Roman cooking at moderate prices, and in northern Rome, **Dai Toscani**, Via Forlì 41 (tel: 862 477) gives the choice of Tuscan or Roman entrées.

Other Italian Cuisine

Eating Italian in Rome can mean from Tuscan to Venetian. A particularly celebrated but expensive restaurant in the

FOOD AND DRINK

Sabatini, with its typically Roman, faded façade, is a popular restaurant serving local dishes

heart of town is **El Toulà**, Via della Lupa 29b (tel: 678 1196) where the emphasis is on Venetian specialities in an elegant setting. Service is impeccable and famous faces are often to be seen. Near Via del Corso Mario, **Via della Vite 55** (tel: 678 3818) will present you with a less expensive bill for Tuscan fare in slightly more rustic surroundings. **Alfreda alla Scrofa**, Via della Scrofa 104 (tel: 654 0163), where the famous *fettucine* was first served, is at the centre of Rome. Equally central but more moderately priced is the popular **La Fontanella**, Largo

Fontanella Borghese 86 (tel: 678 3849), a Tuscan eating place noted for its barbecued meats. Abruzzi dishes (try the tuna fish) are the key to **Abruzzi**, Via del Vaccaro (tel: 679 3897) near the Piazza Venezia. Not far from Termini Station, **Monte Arci**, Via Castelfidardo 33 (tel. 474 4890) is full of character and flavour. In bright **Elettra**, Via Principe Amedeo 72 (tel: 474 5397), on the opposite side of the station, you can try *bucatini alla capricciosa* with a very rich sauce, or lean calf *all abruzzese*.

Seafood
Seafood of some kind is almost always to be found on menus, but does tend to be expensive and those restaurants which highlight it are in the luxury bracket. Such a place is **Alberto Ciarla**, Piazza San Cosimato 40 (tel: 581 8668) in Trastevere, but the seafood is prepared very creatively. Somewhat more reasonable is **L'Orca**, Via GC Santini 12 (tel: 589 1301), and at **Cencia**, Via della Lungaretta 67 (tel: 582 670) complete seafood meals are offered. Famous but pricey **Gino**, Via della Lungaretta (tel: 580 3403) is renowned for its seafood spreads, and summer garden. Near the Via Vittorio Veneto is upmarket **Pinciana**, Via Sardegna 34 (tel: 679 5069) where the seafood is fresh every day, as it is at centrally placed **L'Angoletto**, Piazza Rondanini 51 (tel: 686 1203). **Al Presidente**, Via in Arcione 94 (tel: 679 7342) and **Rosetta**, Via della Rosetta 9 (tel: 656 1002)

near the Pantheon, are also excellent.

International

Renowned enough for its quality to require a reservation, **La Sans Souci**, Via Sicilia 20 (tel: 493 504) is close to the Via Vittorio Veneto and offers high class Italian and international cuisine. In the historic centre, **Passetto**, Via Zanardelli 14 (tel: 654 0569) serves a wide variety of international food with something for everyone, while **Basilica Ulpia**, Via del Foro di Traiano 2 (tel: 679 6271), stands amid the ruins of Trajan's Markets; but it is not cheap.

Ethnic

Frankly, it is foolish to eat anything but Italian in Rome, but if you must, plump for somewhere as famous as **Ranieri**, Via Mario dei Fiori 26 (tel: 679 1592) near the Piazza di Spagna. It was founded in 1865 by a Neopolitan who cooked for Queen Victoria and later for Maximillian's wife, Charlotte. This elegant restaurant with old world appeal gives a French and regal touch to dishes like *Crêpes alla Ranieri, Gnocchetti Parisian* and *tournedos Henry IV*. A pleasant evening with French cuisine and a musical show is possible at **Le Cabanon**, Vicolo della Luce 4 (tel: 581 8106) in Trastevere, and **Charly's Sauciere**, Via di San Giovanni in Laterano, between the basilica and Colosseum (tel: 736 666) is certainly mentionable for its fondue, onion soup and cheese soufflé.

Good Chinese restaurants are rather few and far between but the **Golden Crown**, Via in Arcione 85 (tel: 678 3406) serves Cantonese cuisine which is recommended. Another suggestion is **Hong Kong**, Via Monterone 14 (tel: 654 1687), though for romantic candle-lit dining, you're best off at **Thien Kim**, Via Guilia 201 (tel: 654 7832) where Vietnamese style delicacies include duck with medicinal herbs and fondue.

A penchant for *sachertorte* could lead you to **Wiener Bierhaus**, Via della Croce 22 (tel: 679 5569) where as its name suggests, the food has an Austrian flavour. Typical Viennese dishes, including goulash, can be tried at **Albrecht Pub**, Via F Crispi 39 (tel: 493 439). In the Borgo area, **Taverna Negma**, Borgo Vittorio 92 (tel: 656 5143) is an Arab restaurant serving traditional couscous.

Cheap and Cheerful

If you do not order fish, you can get away with a low bill at **Vincenzo**, Via Castelfidardo 6 (tel: 484 4596) and **Città d'Oro**, Via Nomentana 79 (tel: 855 001) is a cheap Chinese restaurant. **McDonald's** had quite a fight before opening on Piazza di Spagna 45 while near St Peter's **Il Colonnato**, Piazza Sant'Uffizio 7, serves up economical breakfasts and lunches.

Where to Drink

A bar in Rome is not just the place you go for a drink. Most bars are a mixture of pub and café, where you can eat, buy

FOOD AND DRINK

snacks and cigarettes or use the phone. They are social centres where it's not unusual to see under fives sipping milk alongside older customers. The tiniest watering hole is quite prepared to serve coffee and larger establishments may well specialise in ice cream and even have a restaurant area. Prices are cheaper in the stand-up bar, though if you have overdone the sightseeing, look for somewhere with chairs. Generally, at this type of place, you pay before you order, that is you go to the cashier (*cassa*), state what you want and pay for it and use to receipt to reorder and claim your drink from the counter. By and large, Romans are not beer drinkers, but they do like wine. Even the men do not consider it effete to ask for a glass of Castelli Romani, Frascati, Marino, Colli Albani or Velletri, all reputable local wines, palatable when drunk young. They will tell you such wines offer the soothing contrast to their much-loved flavoursome food and even a *vino da tavola* (table wine) served by the jug or carafe, can be quite pleasing.

The classic aperitif is a vermouth, red or white, dry or sweet, with ice and lemon peel, or a campari, served straight, with soda or orange juice. *Punt e Mes* is also popular with Italians because its bitter taste stimulates the appetite, and is considered to be an equally good antidote for a hangover.

Beer Houses

Albrecht, Via F Crispi 39 (tel: 679 8767)

Birreria Bavarese, Via Vittoria 47 (tel: 679 0383)

MEC, Piazza Capranica 76 (tel: 679 3977)

Birreria del West, Piazzale Marconi 32 (EUR) (tel: 591 1458)

Birreria Marconi, Via A Prassede 9c (tel: 486 636)

Birreria Viennese, Via della Croce 21 (tel: 679 5560)

Cantina Tirolese, Via Vitellschi 23 (tel: 656 9994)

SS Apostoli, Piazza SS Apostoli 52 (tel: 678 9032)

Späten Bräu, Viale America 73 (tel: 591 3841)

Café Bars

Allemagna, Via del Corso 181 (tel: 679 2887) has mirrored walls and gilded candelabra. It is large, busy and central and serves as many milk shakes (*frullati*) as it does alcoholic beverages. All rather grand.

Bar San Filippo, Via di Villa San Filippo 8 (tel: 879 314), is more of an ice cream parlour really, and offers a choice of 60 varieties.

Café de Paris, Via Vittorio Veneto 90 (tel: 465 284) has lost some of its previous chic but is air-conditioned, offers courteous service and a good choice of cold snacks, and is open to the early hours.

Doney, Via Vittorio Veneto 145 (tel: 493 407) is situated opposite Café de Paris and has won much of the latter's business. There is also a restaurant here, situated behind the sun terrace.

SHOPPING

Anyone with a taste for the good life will find Rome one of the world's finest shopping centres for luxury goods. Italy's own style and craftsmanship is renowned, and all the other great European names can be found here. If you are looking for quality – and can afford it – this is the place, though bargains might be harder to find.

Naturally, fashions are in the fore, especially in the opulent stores in Via Condotti, Piazza di Spagna, Via Frattina and Via Børgognona, many of which specialise in leather and silk goods. But Rome is also an important centre for jewellery and antiques and ready-to-wear clothes, even if department stores are few and far between as Romans prefer speciality stores.

For those on a tighter budget there are other shopping districts where the financial damage will be less. It is worth investigating Via del Tritone, the streets around the Trevi Fountain, Via Cola di Rienzo across the Tiber, Piazza S Lorenzo in Lucina and the streets around Piazza Campo dei Fiori.

Porta Portese's Sunday market is a mass of colourful stalls and crowds

SHOPPING

Antiques

Serious collectors of antiques should head for Via del Babuino where the grandest shops are located. Look for drawings as well as paintings and furniture at **W Apolloni** (No 133) or *objets d'art* at **Figli di Adolfo di Castro** (No 80), **Nicola e Angelo di Castro** (No 92) or **Amadeo di Castro** (No 77).

Smaller antique shops are found on Via dei Coronari, which were once workshops where artisans crafted rosaries to sell to pilgrims on their way to St Peter's. There are also small antique stores on Via Giulia. Most reputable antique dealers provide a certificate of guarantee *(certificato di garanzia)* and will arrange international shipping.

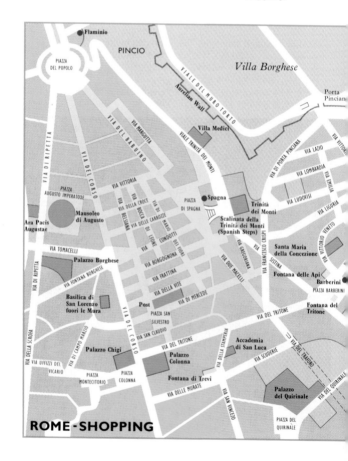

ROME · SHOPPING

Books

Probably the most famous name (and Italy's largest) is **Rizzoli**, Galleria Colonna at Largo Chigi 15. A huge selection of art books often discounted can be found at **Libreria San Silvestro**, Piazza San Silvestro 27. Foreign bookshops include Rome's largest English-language outlet, **Lion Bookshop**, Via del Babuino 181 and the **Anglo-American Book Co**, Via della Vite, 27 and 57. The best place for second-hand paperbacks in English is the **Economy Book Centre**, Piazza di Spagna 29.

Children's Clothes

The name for kids' clothing is **Tablò**, where all the well-heeled mothers buy for well-dressed children. Prices are tottering even for tots at the outlet in Piazza di Spagna 96 (specialising for those under eight), and clothes for the nine years and upwards are available at the other Tablò shop on Via della Croce 84.

China

Some of Italy's finest china comes from **Richard Ginori**, Via Condotti 87, where beautiful table settings are featured on two floors, and **Cavatorta**, Via Veneto 159 which has been selling classic Capodimonte china for over 100 years.

Department Stores

There are some good Italian chain stores although no grand department stores. The best is probably **Coin**, Piazzale Appio, though **Standa** has several branches and is well known. You will find a branch on Via del Corso 379, and one in **Prati** on Via Cola di Rienzo 173. The most central branch of **UPIM** is at Largo Tritone 172 – unexciting but cheap.

Fabrics

The city's largest collection of dress and furnishing fabrics can be found in a setting to match – the 17th-century palatial former home of

You can enjoy a stroll along Via Condotti, even without spending money in its smart shops

Cardinal Altieri before he became Pope Clement X. At **Bises**, Via del Gesù 93 you will find an amazingly wide range of materials. Also prestigious is **Cesari**, housed in another old palace, which has the largest assortment of decorative fabrics in Rome at Via del Babuino 16 and a wonderful stock of linens in its outlet at Via Barberini 1.

Fashions and Accessories

This is the area where Rome comes into its own. True shoppers will hardly know where to start! **Armani** is one of the best designers of Italian ready-to-wear clothing and you can see his latest collections at Via del Babuino 102, while further ahead in the direction of Piazza del Popolo, **Emporio Armani** features teenage clothes. Via Frattina is the place for younger fashion and at **Alexander**, on the corner of Piazza di Spagna, you can see the very latest. For men, one of the best known tailors is **Angelo Litrico**, Via Sicilia 51, or for a custom-made suit, Italian styled and ready within two days, try **D'Alesio Tailoring. André Laug**, Piazza di Spagna 81 creates classically-styled shirts. **Battistoni**, Via Condotti 61, is a luxurious boutique that sells rugs and equestrian prints as well as the most refined cashmere sweaters, blazers, elegant articles of silk, linen, wool, corduroy and leather, though undoubtedly some of his customers these days have been wooed away by family tailor, **Cucci**, Via Condotti 67 who supplies Alain Delon among others. Also try **Caraceni**, Via Sardegna 50, or **Carlo Palazzi** on Via Borgognona where extraordinary fabrics are used for suits and overcoats.

If your taste is for the less conventional visit **Filippo**, Via Condotti 6, who creates the trendiest clothes in Rome. Prices are high but ideas are up to the minute. **Fendi**, on the Via Borgognona, is one of the big Italian names for luxury purchases, another is **Gasbarri**, Via Condotti 38, whose windows are dedicated to classic high fashion. On the Via Borgognona, **Gianfranco Ferre** shows off men's fashions for every occasion and **Gianni Versace** offers some very original men's pyjamas. **Givenchy** is on the same street.

Ungaro (a tailor with a particular philosophy who has become prophet for Parisienne haute couture) has a boutique at Via Bocca di Leone 24' where his classic silk dresses and wool suits (made in Italy) cost less than in Paris, and finally **Valentino** has a men's boutique on Via Mario de' Fiori 22 (selling understated suits and monogrammed jewellery and belts) and boutiques on Via Bocca di Leone 15 and Via Gregoriana 24.

Leather

Almost all the big names in Rome sell some leather items, including **Trussardi**, Via Bocca di Leone 27, who has established a good reputation for his unique style of leather accessories, although Romans consider **Nazareno Gabrielli**, Via Sant'Andrea delle Fratte 3a, more or less the inventor of leather and tweed outfits. Sturdy goodlooking leather suitcases are the *pièce de résistance* at **Etienne Aigner**, Via San Sebastianello 7, whose symbols and house initials form a horseshoe. **Maurizio Righini**, an experienced leather goods dealer, has had his shop in the centre of Rome since 1930. You will find it at Piazza di Spagna 36. Every type of leather item is available at **Elegant Belamonte**, Via Emilia 36, and if you are looking for gloves, set off immediately for **Sergio di Cori**, Piazza di Spagna 53.

Jewellery

Jewels for the royals are made at **Bulgari**, behind the portals of Via Condotti 10. Naturally, the prices are more than princely. In Via Borgognona, **Sutrini** continues to make wonderful creations, using combinations of metals and industrial materials with gold and precious stones. On the same street, **Gris** stocks unusual jewellery – 40s-style platinum and diamond hairpins or a miniature Van Cleef watch. Antique precious watches are the speciality of a shop which is a newcomer to this street, **Bolla**.

SHOPPING

Rome's oldest market, the Campo dei Fiori, specialises in selling fresh food and flowers

Shoes

When a visitor to Rome plans to splurge, as often as not it will be on shoes. Comfort and quality are the trademark of shoes at **Rossetti** on Via Borgognona. On the same street, **Andrea Carrano** houses shoes in all colours and shades for every occasion and at No 38, **Maud Frizon**'s boutique has some strikingly original designs in fun colours. **Gucci** moccasins are so popular they're almost passé – there are two Gucci shops on Via Condotti and one on Via Borgognona. **Ferragamo** on Via

Condotti 66, is one of the most classic names for fashion parade shoes, but also look in at **Barrila** at No 29. And who can resist the dainty, sparkling evening shoes at **Beltrami** Via Condotti 19?

Markets

Even the wealthy shop for food and flowers in Rome's markets and the not so rich may well find an inexpensive item of clothing or leather. The city's oldest market is the **Campo dei Fiori**, open daily except Sunday in the heart of Rome. The **Mercato dei Fiori** is dedicated to nothing but flowers, but it is only open to the public on a Tuesday, from 10.30 to 13.00 hrs. You will find it in a covered hall on Via Trionfale in the district of Prati. Flowers can be bought day or night in Via L Mercantini, near the Gianicolo, and at the start of Via Angelol Emo.

Rome's largest market is the one which stretches around the edge of the huge **Piazza Vittorio Emanuele** every day but Sunday. There are clothes and leather goods ranged along one side, food along the other. The atmosphere is lively and entertaining and it is a good place to pick up unusual cheeses and salad vegetables for a picnic lunch. Go early on Sunday morning to **Porta Portese**, Ponte Sublicio close to the Tiber in Trastevere. This flea market is very popular and always crowded but it is fun and often full of strolling musicians. Porta Portese opens at 06.30 hrs and closes at 14.30 hrs on Sundays only.

ACCOMMODATION

When it comes to
accommodation there are two
points to note. First, do not
judge by the exterior as many
a crumbling façade has a
palatial interior. Second, be
prepared for noise almost
wherever you stay. Another
point might be not to save
money by staying out of the
centre at the cost of time.
Having said that, Rome, like
any other capital, offers a full
range of accommodations from
the low cost *pensione*, usually
small, family-run hostelries
offering bed and breakfast or
half board rates, to the
grandest of palaces which
have become some of
Europe's finest hotels. Italy
uses the star system to classify
its hotels with ratings of one to
five stars. Self-catering flatlets
are available in what are
called *Residences*, but for
these you should obtain a list
from the Italian State Tourist
Office. The largest numbers of
first class and fashionable
hotels are to be found around
the Via Vittorio Veneto and the
Piazza di Spagna, while more
pensione are located in the
Borgo and Prati. The area
around the central railway
station can be rather seedy but
a few hotels here have
maintained their standards and
the *albergo diurno* or day hotel
at the station is a useful place
to freshen up. Rome's peak
season is between Easter and
October, but although many
hotels feature off-season rates
between November and
March, the city always seems

to be well booked, so advance
reservations really are
essential.

Luxury (Five Star)
Some would say that from a
prestigious point of view the
Hassler-Villa Medici, Piazza
Trinità dei Monti 6 (tel: 678
2651) is the best. It does have a
fantastic position, above the
Spanish Steps with views over
the city from many of its rooms,
and the decor inside suggests
quiet affluence which is what
this hotel is all about. Its Roof
Restaurant offers excellent
Italian and international cuisine
and breakfast in the garden in
summer is a delight. Five other
deluxe hotels within the Via

*In a city of elegance, the Hassler-
Villa Medici hotel sets the pace*

ACCOMMODATION

Vittorio Veneto area are:
Ambasciatori Palace, Via
Vittorio Veneto 70 (tel 474 93)
thankfully with soundproofed
rooms and service as
impeccable as ever. Its ABC
Grill Bar gets good ratings. The
much loved and venerated
Excelsior (part of the Cigahotels
group), Via Vittorio Veneto 125
(tel: 4708) is a splendid grand
hotel furnished with antiques,
and with a good piano bar. The
long-established **Eden**, Via
Ludovisi 49 (tel: 474 3551)
possibly offers the lowest rates
in the luxury bracket. The
Bernini Bristol, Piazza Barberini
23 (tel: 463 051) faces Bernini's
Triton Fountain and is within
walking distance of the Spanish
Steps. Behind its neo-classical
façade, **The Grand** (Cigahotels),
Via Vittorio Emanuele Orlando 3
(tel: 4709) is indeed an oasis of
grandeur that has always
attracted the élite, with the
notable Rallye Restaurant for
haute cuisine. **Lord Byron**, Via G
de Notaris in Parioli district (tel:
360 9541) is a quiet, exclusive
retreat just outside of the centre
– a place to stay for those who
wish to be private. Also further
from the middle of Rome, but
still in the luxury bracket, is the
Cavalieri Hilton, Via Cadlolo 101
(tel: 31511) which enjoys a
splendid panorama.

First Class (Four Star)
Hotel de la Ville, Via Sistina 69
(tel: 6733) is next to the Hassler
so it is popular with shoppers
and has a good restaurant,
Il Patio. Ernest Hemingway,
Henry James and host of other
celebrities have stayed at
Hotel d'Inghilterra, Via Bocca

*Luxury is the predominant feature
of the neo-classical Grand hotel*

di Leone 14 (tel: 672 161) which
has been open since 1850. This
century's improvements have
included air conditioning and
colour TVs. The stylish
Raphael, Largo Febo 2 (tel: 650
881), near the Piazza Navona
conceals *objets d'art* behind its
vine-covered walls and
politicians often drop in as
Parliament stands opposite.
Two other comfortable first
class hotels are the **Colonna
Palace**, Piazza di Montecitorio
12 (tel: 678 1341) and the
Nazionale, Piazza Montecitorio
131 (tel: 678 9251).
In the Via Veneto area the
Flora, Via Vittorio Veneto 191
(tel: 497 821) is an old
fashioned hotel with traditional
service; also recommended

are the **Majestic** at No 50 (tel: 486 841), and **Regina Carlton** at No 72 (tel: 476 851). At the nearby **Etap Boston**, Via Limbardia 47 (tel: 473 951) the rates include breakfast. **The Savoia**, Via Ludovisi 15 (tel: 474 4141) has sterling virtues that befit its solid exterior. Tucked away, a quiet street facing the Aurelian Wall, the **Victoria**, Via Campania 41 (tel: 473 931) has good views from its upper rooms over the Villa Borghese and the modern interior of the **Londra & Cargill**, Piazza Sallustio 18 (tel: 473 871) belies any anonymity its façade might suggest.

In the Prati district, the **Giulio Cesare**, Via degli Scipioni 287 (tel: 310 244) has the ambience of turn-of-the-century decor with modern amenities. Nearby, the **Jolly Leonardo da Vinci**, Via dei Gracchi 324 (tel: 39680) is good value. Recommended for the station area is the **Atlantico**, Via Cavour 23 (tel: 485 951); the **Genova**, Via Cavour 33 (tel: 476 951) or the **Massimo d'Azeglio**, Via Cavour 18 (tel: 460 646) which has refused to be overcome by the dilapidation of the area. Also worth considering is the **Mediterraneo**, Via Cavour 15 (tel: 464 051) or the **Mondial**, Via Torino 127 (tel: 472 861).

Second Class (or Three Star)
Unpretentious as the **Condotti**, Via Mario de'Fiori (tel: 679 4661) is, it has a prime location near the high-priced shops of the Via Condotti and in its rooms with small terraces, it is easy to watch the well-heeled go by. Of equal standard is the **Internazionale**, Via Sistina 79 (tel: 679 3047) and the **Sistina**, Via Sistina 136 (tel: 475 8867) which has a lovely summer breakfast terrace. On Via Vittorio Veneto, the **Alexandra**, Via Vittorio Veneto 18 (tel: 461 943) does charge above average for this location but its air of faded gentility appeals to some. In the same neighbourhood, the **Caprice**, Via Liguria 38 (tel: 460 779) is an alternative. **The Marcella**, Via Flavia 106 (tel: 474 6206) includes breakfast, has a splendid view from its Roof Garden and boasts a solarium. Not too far from St Peter's in the Prati area, the **Diplomatic**, Via Vittoria Colonna 28 (tel: 654 2084) is popular and so is the completely renewed **Isa**, Via Cicerone 30 (tel: 380 253).

ACCOMMODATION

Housed in an impressive building, the centrally situated Hotel dei Portoghesi has a special appeal

Other Hotels

The City, Vie Due Macelli (tel: 679 7468) includes breakfast in its rates and is in fact a 17th-century palace with a family atmosphere. Air conditioning is 'upon request' but the panoramic terrace is magnificent at the **Hotel dei Portoghesi**, Via dei Portoghesi 1 (tel: 658 4231) which sits on an attractive street next to the church of S Antonio. This small hotel has a central position, and although no longer cheap, is still excellent value.

Residences

Those planning a lengthier stay in Rome may prefer a *Residence* or rental flat. Among those recommended are: the **Palazzo al Velabro**, Via del Velabro 16 (tel: 679 4325) which offers one, two or three room apartments for a seven-night minimum stay with daily cleaning. Near St Peter's, the **Aurelia Antica**, Via Aurelia Antica 425 (tel: 637 9021) offers something similar. The **Medaglie d'Oro**, Via Medaglie d'Oro, (tel: 359 9051) demands a fortnight's stay minimum and charges extra for use of TV or laundry. One month's stay is the minimum at the **Monti Parioli** in the Parioli area, Via Torquato Tarameili 4 (tel: 870 644) but this does include 24-hour porter service and daily cleaning.

Camping

It sounds ridiculous for a stay in Rome, but you might like to consider camping. Rome has a number of sites in its surrounds, mostly equipped with water, electricity and toilet facilities. It is inadvisable to camp outside official sites. Recommended sites include: **Seven Hills**, Via Cassia 1216, La Maggiolina (tel: 376 5571). Capacity 600; Bungalows. **Capitol**, Ostia Antica (near Sassone), 45, Via Castellusano (tel: 660 2301). Capacity 1,800. **Lorium**, Via Aurelia (tel: 690 9190; 690 9189). **Flaminio**, Via Flaminia Nuova (tel: 327 9008). **Nomentano**, Via della Cesarina (tel: 610 0296). Capacity 700. **Tiber**, Via Tiberina, Prima Porta (tel: 691 0733).

NIGHTLIFE AND ENTERTAINMENT

Rome gets sleepier earlier than say Paris or New York and is not a city which can, or wants to, boast about sleazy clubs like Hamburg, despite Fellini movies. But that does not mean there are no late night revellers here nor a shortage of clubs and discos which pump out music through the small hours. Indeed, theatres and restaurants tend to keep quite late hours and cafés and bars usually do not close before 01.00 or 02.00 am even on weekdays.

There is something for everyone in Rome after dark and naturally, being the cultural city it is, the more highbrow types of entertainment – opera, ballet, recitals, concerts and theatre – which feature prominently. One of the great summer attractions is open-air opera in the fantastic setting of the ancient Baths of Caracalla, but equally, summer sees a vibrant jazz, pop and rock festival taking place in Rome's parks and gardens. Orchestral music, including the Accademia Filarmonica can be heard in a variety of venues, almost all centrally located as are the theatres. Yes, you will need a good knowledge of Italian to understand Pirandello, a staple at established theatres, and only the bi-lingual should attempt to attend fringe theatre *(teatri off)*, a lot of which is too political and controversial to be considered pleasurable by many visitors.

If you know a little Italian, it might just be worth honing in at the cinema. Most of the films shown in Italy these days are foreign made (often American) but they are dubbed in Italian. Only one brave cinema currently runs films with their original soundtrack though Romans themselves will tell you they'd prefer to see undubbed films with just subtitles for guidance. One of the great summer events is a series of Italian and foreign films projected in the open at some ancient monument. Fast food stalls add to the festive air. In Rome, the words 'nightclub' and 'discotheque' are almost interchangeable, so beware that the aim of some is to part the tourist from as much of his money as is possible in the shortest amount of time. Some establishments charge an entrance fee which includes a drink; others allow free entry but price the drinks higher. Most clubs close during stretches of summer.

The best sources of entertainment information are to be found in the Friday edition of *Il Messaggero*, the Friday supplement of *La Repubblica* and the tourist publications, *This Week in Rome* and *A Guest in Rome*. Tickets for most cultural performances may be purchased from the various box offices right up to the day of performance but credit cards are not accepted.

Opera and Ballet

The main venue for both opera and ballet is **Teatro**

dell'Opera, Piazza Beniamino Gigli 1 (tel: 46364) with an official season from November–June. Reservations for performances have to be made by mail (direct or through a travel agent) but any unsold tickets go on sale two days before any given performance (the box office is closed on Mondays). Open air summer productions (from June to September) are given at the Baths of Caracalla, Via delle Terme di Caracalla (tel: 575 8300). Tickets for these may be purchased at the Teatro dell' Opera box office or at the Baths on the day of performance from 20.00 to 21.00 hrs.

Classical concerts and recitals

The official concert season runs from October–June although concerts, choral recitals and chamber music can be heard throughout the year in a variety of splendid settings like the Basilica of S Giovanni in Laterano, and in summer at the Basilica of Maxentius, Via dei Fori Imperali (tel: 679 3617), or at villas like Villa Ada. One of the most famous hosts to international concert stars is the Accademia di Santa Cecilia which holds concerts in the Auditorio di Via della Conciliazione, (tel: 654 1044) and at the Sala Accademica di Via dei Greci (tel: 679 0389). The Accademia Filarmonica, Via Flaminia 118 (tel: 360 1752) frequently performs at the Teatro Olimpico on Piazza Gentile da Fabriano 17 (tel: 396

2635) and the RAI Italian radio orchestra generally uses Foro Italico, Piazza Lauro de Bosis (tel: 390 713). Other city concert halls include Auditorio Pio, Via della Conciliazione 4 (tel: 651 4044); Auditorio del San Leone Magno, Via Bolzano 38 (tel: 853 216) and the Auditorio del Gonfalone, Via del Gonfalone 32a (tel: 655 952).

Modern music and jazz

The best place for jazz is the Mississippi Jazz Club, Borgo Angelico 16 (tel: 654 0348), but jazz is often featured at the various summer festivals or in October at the Teatro dell'Opera (check the local papers and tourist guides). The recommended place to listen to folk music is Folkstudio, Via Gaetano Sacchi 3 (tel: 589 2374). Big rock concerts are often staged at Castel Sant'Angelo and Stadio Olimpico. Fans of jazz, folk and pop music might also check out the following: Il Pipistrello, Via Emilia 27a (tel: 475 4123); El Trauco, Via Fonte dell'Olio 5 (tel: 589 5928); Saint Louis Music City, Via del Cardello 13a (tel: 474 5076); Murales, Via dei Fienaroli 30 (tel: 589 8844); Music-Inn, Largo dei Fiorentini 3 (tel: 654 4934); Music Workshop, Via Prati 19 (tel: 844 1886).

Nightclubs and discos

The closest thing to a cabaret/revue club is Fantasie di Trastevere, Via di Santa Dorotea 6 (tel: 589 1671). It is designed for tourists and you will have to suffer indifferent food if you want to see the

Good to namedrop: the Jackie O disco

show. One of the most famous discotheques is **Piper 80**, Via Tagliamento 9 (tel: 854 459) which has a young atmosphere. If you just want to say you have been there, **Jackie O**, Via Boncompagni 11 (tel: 461 401) is still going even though its glorious past is past. Another traditional establishment is the classic **Club 84**, Via Emilia 84 (tel: 475 1538) with an orchestra and disco music. A very large elegant disco is **Histeria**, Via R Giovannelli (tel: 864 587) and a very large loud disco is **Acropolis**, Via L Luciani 52 (tel: 870 504) which offers fast food, a video gallery and conversation corners. Youth, elegance and exclusivity is to be found at **Le Stelle**, Via C

Beccaria 22 (tel: 361 1240) but if you want loud new wave rock music, **Supersonic** is the place for you, Via Ovidio 17 (tel: 654 8435). **Oscar Club**, Via Principessa Clotide 11 (tel: 361 0284) has an international patronage perhaps because it has been designed as a New York style club with an American bar, restaurant and music. **Veleno**, Via Sardegna 27 (tel: 493 583), is an extravagant discotheque and restaurant furnished with antique Roman furniture.
A number of nightclub/discos are more like piano bars. At **Bella Blu**, for example, Via L Luciani 21 (tel: 360 8840) they still dance cheek to cheek on a small dance floor surrounded by star-sprinkled blue walls and Ionic pilasters. **La Biblioteca**, too, is romantic –

you can dine and dance until late here: Largo del Teatro Valle 27 (tel: 654 1292). **Bluebar** and **La Cabala**, Via dei Soldati 25 (tel: 656 4250) atop Hostaria dell'Orso saw a lot of Onassis's passion – first for Maria Callas and then for Jackie Kennedy. Today, it is posh and expensive and still exciting for some. Rather more reserved is **La Clef**, Via March 13 (tel: 461 730). At **Open Gate**, Via San Nicola da Tolentino (tel: 474 6301) there's a piano bar, restaurant and smart disco and at **Tartarughino**, Via della Scrofa 2 (tel: 6786037) you can listen to piano and classical guitars. The spread in popularity of Latin American rhythms has come to Rome as much as to other European capitals. Brazilian music is big, for instance at **L'Incontro**, Via della Penna 25 (tel: 361 0934) and at **Yes Brazil**, Via S Francesco a Ripa 103 (tel: 581 6267) you can sip batida cocktails and tropical fruit milk shakes all day and all night. Beware that nightspots do have a habit of appearing and disappearing at an alarming rate.

Gay Discos

Rome has its fair share of gay nightspots. Among the best are **L'Alibi**, Via Monte Testaccio 44 (tel: 578 2343) which is expensive with a young crowd. **Easy Going**, Via della Purificazione 9 (tel: 474 5578) is liked by models of both sexes and is easy going enough not to refuse entry to straights. **L'Angelo Azzurro**, Via Cardinal Merry Del Val (tel: 580 0472) is currently trendy with the young crowd. **L'Incognito**, Via Vincenze 58a (tel: 492 401) will let you in if you show a foreign passport.

Cinema

The only cinema which shows films in their original versions is **Pasquino**, Piazza Santa Maria in Trastevere (tel: 580 3622), otherwise you will need a good knowledge of Italian, as most films are dubbed. However, the art cinema clubs are worth investigating since they may be joined on the spot for a nominal fee and often present European and American art films undubbed as well as rock movies and other films made by young, independent Italian film makers. Check out the following: **Farnese**, Piazza Campo dei Fiori 56 (tel: 656 4395); **Filmstudio**, Via Orti d'Alibert 1c (tel: 657 378); **Il Labirinto**, Via Pompeo Magno 27 (tel: 312 283); **Grauco Cinema**, Via Perugia 34 (tel: 755 1785); **Cavalieri del Nulla**, Via della Baleari 167 (tel: 759 1377), **L'Officina**, Via Benaco 3 (tel: 862 530); **Sala Borgo**, Borgo S Angelo 19 (tel: 358 5548). In August, films are shown in the open air at the Arch of Constantine or some other ancient monument. For a small fee, you can see as many as five films at one sitting right through to almost breakfast time.

Theatre

Officially, the theatre season runs from October to May, although, in the summer months, open-air performances are given outside Rome at classical sites such as Ostia Antica. The lightest programmes are to be found at **Bagaglino al Salone Margherita**, Vie Due Macelli 75 (tel: 654 4601) which is more cabaret style and serves drinks besides or the **Sistina**, Via Sistina 129 (tel: 475 6841) which stages musicals. If you appreciate classic theatre and can understand Italian, look to the following:

Anfitrione, Via S Saba 24 (tel: 575 0827). **Argentina**, Largo Argentina (tel: 654 4601). **Belli**, Piazza S Aplolonia 11a (tel: 589 4875). **Dei Satiri**, Via di Grotta Pinta 19 (tel: 656 1311). **Dei Servi**, Via del Mortaro 22 (tel: 679 5130). **Delle Arti**, Via Sicilia 59 (tel: 475 8598). **Delle Muse**, Via Forlì 43 (tel: 862 948). **Eliseo**, Via Nazionale 183 (tel: 462 114). **Flaiano**, Via S Stefano del Cacco 15 (tel: 679 8569).

Ghione, Via delle Fornaci 37 (tel: 637 2294). **Giulio Cesare**, Viale G Cesare 229 (tel: 384 454). **Goldoni**, Vicolo de'Soldati 4 (tel: 656 1156). **Nuovo Parioli**, Via Giosuè Borsi 20 (tel: 396 2635). **Olimpico**, Piazza Gentile da Fabriano (tel: 396 2635). **Politecnico**, Via G B Tiepolo 13a (tel: 360 7559). **Quirino**, Via Marco Minghetti 1 (tel: 679 4585). **Ridotto dell'Eliseo**, Via Nazionale 183 (tel: 465 095). **Rossini**, Piazza di Santa Chiara 14 (tel: 654 2770). **Sala Umberto**, Via della Mercede 50 (tel: 679 4753). **Valle**, Via del Teatro Valle (tel: 654 3794). **Teatro dell'Orologio**, Via dei Filippini 17a (tel: 654 8735). **Teatro Tenda**, Piazza Mancini (tel: 393 969).

The Piazza del Popolo: Rome by night is a theatre in itself

WEATHER AND WHEN TO GO

If one can ever generalise about the weather, you might say that Rome is usually mild and pleasant. Even winter temperatures are pretty moderate, *but* it can be freezing cold and wet in January and February despite an average indication of around 4°C (40°F) in those months. It is also certain that while the average July and August temperatures read in the high 20sC (80sF), the city can get extremely hot, sticky and humid and reach the 30sC (90sF).

What Clothes to Bring

The Romans are stylish without being over formal, so in most places, ties and evening dress are unnecessary. Lightweight cottons are the obvious summer choice, but remember that short skirts, shorts and bare arms are not acceptable in churches. In winter, you may well want a warm coat and umbrella. At any time of year, Rome is hard on the feet, so comfortable shoes are essential and comfortable dress of all kinds is best suited to sightseeing.

When to Go

Everyone will tell you that the best time of year in Rome is the spring or autumn and common sense will tell you the city is at its most crowded during July and August.

The sunny Piazza della Rotonda. The pace of life in summer is relaxed – especially for visitors

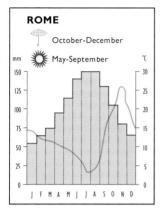

ROME

October-December

May-September

HOW TO BE A LOCAL

If you drive like a maniac, gesticulate with passion, adore endless cups of coffee as you people-watch outdoors, you might pass for a local. The Romans, like all Italians, appreciate a good argument and love a receptive audience. They are vain, but smart, reserving most of their scorn for each other, not foreigners. (The competitive spirit between Romans and Venetians is a long standing one.) They are cheerful and helpful as a rule – less excitable and more courteous and reserved than in other parts of Italy. From clothes to behaviour, appearance is all; being drunk in public is seen as the height of ugliness. And though young Roman men pursue attractive foreign girls as diligently as ever, they are easily put in their place and are unlikely to pinch bottoms these days. Like all Italians, the Romans love children, and they have an ambivalent attitude towards the Church, somehow managing to combine irreverence with reverence.

PERSONAL PRIORITIES

Rome is one of the world's great capital cities, and there is nothing that cannot be bought here. You will have no trouble in obtaining whatever kind of pharmaceutical or baby care products you require, and you will find that it is easy to obtain brands which are familiar names in many other countries, including *Tampax* and *Pampers* (*pannolini*); the Swedish brand *Lines* is also very popular. Cotton wool is *cotone* and condoms are *preservativi*. Although the days are gone when any female bottom was likely to be pinched, women without male companions may still find themselves the subject of unwelcome attentions, but not usually enough to be a serious problem.

The biggest threat by far in Rome is from bag snatchers. These thieves are *very* skilled – so be particularly careful with hand baggage. Don't carry large sums of cash or wear obviously expensive jewellery. The Old Quarter of Rome is a very popular area, both with visitors and with the whole range of Roman society: so it is not necessarily the place for privacy and contemplation, but it is lively.

Finally, on a safety note, everything you've heard about Italian drivers is true – so unless you really need to, don't cross the road!

CHILDREN

If the children get bored and tired of monuments, take a break and buy them an ice cream – Rome sells some of the best in the world (see 'Food and Drink', page 85). Italians spoil their children, and the city boasts plenty of toy shops which will enchant your own and several cinemas and theatres stage shows specifically for the kids. Most of the outdoor activities are centred in the piazzas – especially Navona in December and January when there is a market and carnival celebrations – and the parks, of which the city has many. Children always delight in tossing coins into Trevi Fountain or taking a horse-drawn carriage ride from the base of the Spanish Steps and, given an interesting guide, no doubt be enthralled with major landmarks like the Colosseum. As a last resort, buy them the Italian comic, *Topolino*, which is published weekly.

Parks and Zoos

Number one attraction is the permanent amusement park at EUR, Via delle Tre Fontane (tel: 592 5933) known as **Luna Park**. It is very large and well equipped with all kinds of attractions including a big wheel and roller coaster and the thrills of the Himalaya Railroad. This is a family amusement park so there is plenty to do, including attractions such as boating lake, miniature golf course, cafés and bars.

Far less impressive but still worth consideration is the small fairground in **Parco Oppio**, north of the Colosseum (entered from Via Labicana) and the carousels and roller rink in the gardens of the **Ministero degli Affari Esteri**, Piazzale della Farnesina. The **Villaggio Olimpico**, not far from Corso di Francia also has a roller skating rink and a playground. One of the best Rome parks for energetic children is **Villa Ada**, west of Via Salaria, where they will find two playgrounds, a roller rink, areas for biking, ponds and wooded slopes. Pony rides are given in **Villa Glori**, north of Villa Borghese, and pony cart rides in **Villa Balestra**. Trastevere's **Villa Sciarra** is a much smaller park with an aviary, and **Villa Celimontana**, south of the Colosseum, has a cycle track. In much loved Villa Borghese you can rent a boat or visit the well-maintained little **Giardino Zoologico** (tel: 870 564). The zoo is open all year (except 1 May), 08.00–18.15 hrs in summer; 08.00–17.00 hrs in winter, with free admission for children. Check the feeding times posted near the entrance. The nearest safari park is close to Fiumicino Airport, Via Portuense (tel: 601 1188), open Wednesday–Monday 10.30 to just before sunset, but of course this is some way out of the city. So too is the large bird sanctuary run by the World Wide Fund for Nature at Palo (tel: 991 1641), open Thursday–Sunday from 09.30 to sunset.

Theatres and Shows

Puppet shows are a popular
Italian attraction which have an
international appeal, and can
sometimes be seen in Villa
Borghese and in Gianicolo
Park; check local press. They
are also frequently given at
Alla Ringhiera, Via dei Riari 81
(tel: 656 8711).

Other theatres in Rome which
stage special productions for
children from time to time
include: **Il Torchio**, Via E
Morosini 16 (tel: 582 049);
Anteprima, Via Capo d'Africa
5a (tel: 736 255); **Arcobalena**,
Salita S Gregorio al Celio 3 (tel:
732 853); **Catacombe 2000**, Via
Iside 21 (tel: 765 3495); **La
Ciliegia**, Via Giambattista Soria
13 (tel: 627 5705); **Il Giardino
Segreto**, Via Panettoni 67 (tel:
365 0938) and **Laboratorio al
Parco**, Via Ramazzini 31 (tel:
528 0647).

Among other attractions there
is a children's cinema at Viale
della Pineta 15 (tel: 863 485)
and a planetarium is situated
on Via Giuseppe Romita.

Museums

Depending upon tastes, age
and interests, there is plenty to
keep kids happy in Rome's
museums.

The musically inclined
children could well benefit
from a visit to **Museo Nazionale
degli Strumenti Musicali**,
Piazza Santa Croce in
Gerusalemme 9a (tel: 757 5936)
– which displays thousands of
musical instruments dating
from ancient times to the 17th
century.

Open: daily 09.00–13.30 hrs
except Monday.

*One of Italy's contributions to
international cuisine: the pizza*

TIGHT BUDGET

You can keep within a tight
budget in Rome, though at first
it might not look easy. The
main **youth hostel** is at the Foro
Italico 61, Via dell Olimpiade
(but you must be a YHA
member to stay there). Using
public transport to get around
is economical, especially if you
buy the tourist passes, valid for
unlimited travel for specific
periods, and students and
foreign visitors can buy, for a
nominal charge, a free pass
(valid for a year) to all state-
owned museums and galleries,
upon application to the tourist
office in their country of origin.
Remember that stand-up bars
are cheaper than sit-down
ones and that a glass of wine
costs about the same as a
coffee. Fast food outlets and

pizzarias are going to be the cheapest places to eat, especially if they are off the main tourist routes. Otherwise, look for a fixed price menu in an hosteria or trattoria, or make your selection at the snack bar known as a *tavola calda*.

There are several flea markets where you might pick up something new cheaply – early on a Sunday at Porta Portese perhaps or on other mornings at the smaller market in Via Sannio (see 'Shopping', p 91).

FESTIVALS AND EVENTS

January

New Year's Day candlelit procession in the Catacombs of Priscilla.

January 6: carnival on Piazza Navona to mark Epiphany *(Befana)* which carries on until dawn.

January 17: celebrations for the feast of S Antonio.

January 18: St Peter the Apostle celebrations.

January 21: S Agnese festival.

February

The traditional month for Carnival is not really celebrated in Rome though there may be children's parades. Dates and places will be listed in the local press.

March

March 9: Festival of S Francesca; Romans drive their cars to the Piazzale del Colosseo, near the Church of Santa Francesca, for blessing.

March 19: Festival of S Giuseppe which includes

sporting and musical events held in the Trionfale Quarter.

April

Festa della Primavera (Spring Festival) when the Spanish Steps are decorated with pink azaleas and concerts are held in Trinita dei Monti.

Holy Week events include the Procession of the Cross from the Colosseum to the Palatine Hill on Good Friday, led by the Pope, and on Easter Sunday, a traditional papal blessing from the balcony of St Peter's.

April 21: Colourful pageantry for the anniversary of the birth of Rome, held in Piazza del Campidoglio.

May

May Day celebrations.

May 6: Swearing in for the new guard at the Vatican on the anniversary of the Sacking of Rome.

Corpos Domini festival when a street is laid with floral carpets in elaborate motifs.

On the last weekend in May, there is a mounted military parade at Piazza di Siena in Villa Borghese and on Whitsunday a pilgrimage of penitence to the Sanctuary of the Madonna at Castel di Leva a few miles south of Rome.

June

On the first Sunday in June a military parade *(Festa della Repubblica)* centres on Via dei Fori Imperiali.

Festival of S Giovanni.

June 29: Festival of St Peter, Rome's most important religious festival with rites in St Peter's.

During June (to September),

there are many open-air events, including concerts, ballet and theatre, cinema in the open and folklore exhibitions, collectively known as *Estate Romana*.

July
Castel Madama parade in 16th-century costume and horse races.
July 4: American celebrations in Rome including a picnic and fireworks.
Festa de Noiantri, an ancient folklore festivity, happens in the second half of July in Trastevere including processions and entertainment.
Estate Romana (see June).

August
Open-air film festival.
August 5: *Festa della Madonna della Neve* held at Santa Maria Maggiore.
Estate Romana (see June).

September
In early September a harvest festival takes place in the Basilica of Maxentius in the Roman Forum. During the last week of the month a crafts show takes place in Via dell'Orso.
Estate Romana (see June).

November
November 22: Feast of S Cecilia.

December
December 8: *Festa della Madonna Immacolata* (Feast of the Immaculate Conception) in Piazza di Spagna.
Children's market in Piazza Navona.
Christmas celebrations include many masses and Papal blessing.

SPORT AND LEISURE

The 'Great Outdoors' for a Roman can mean a splash in an ancient fountain or a plate of *fettucine* in a garden restaurant. Rome, after all, is no beach resort, though it does boast several parks, one of the most popular being the vast Villa Borghese. Palatine Hill is a good spot for fresh air – and history. Trees and garden shrubbery give the park-like atmosphere; archeological remains, the interest. According to legend, it was here that Romulus traced out the city boundaries in 753 BC. Whether or not you believe that myth, it is a pleasant place for a picnic.

There's no better pastime than a good book in the Villa Borghese

SPORT

Participation Sports
Bicycling
Serious cyclists will find the Olympic cycle track (Velodromo Olympico) at Via della Tecnica, and other race tracks at Villa Celimontana, south of the Colosseum and at Villa Sciarra in Trastevere.

Boating
Rowing boats may be rented at the Giardino del Lago in the Villa Borghese. Several sailing clubs are located at Lake Bracciano, some 30 miles (50 km) from the city and international sailing championships take place at Castel Gandolfo, on Lake Albano, 15 miles (25 km) away.

Bowling
The best of the *bocciodromi* (bowling alleys) are Bowling Brunswick, Via dell'Acqua Acetosa, and Bowling Roma, Viale Regina Margherita 191.

Golf
There are two 18-hole courses – Acqua Santa, Via Appia Nuova and Olgiata, Largo Olgiata 15.

Riding
The Riding Club, Via di Tor Carbone (tel: 542 3998) is your best bet for a single riding session.

Swimming
Some hotels, such as the Cavalieri Hilton, have their own swimming pool. The major outdoor ones in Rome are to be found at the major sports centres – Foro Italico, Lungotevere Maresciallo Cadorna, and Swimming Pool delle Rose at Viale America,

EUR are open from June to September. Foro Italico also has an indoor pool, open from November to May. Sulphur-water swimming (with health in mind) is possible at the Terme Acqua Albule, Bagni di Tivoli, 13 miles (22 km) outside of Rome.

Tennis
Some hotels have their own courts. Public ones are to be found at EUR, Viale dell'Artigianato 2 (tel: 592 4693), Foro Italico (tel: 361 9021), Tennis Belle Arti, Via Flaminia 158 (tel: 360 0602) and Tre Fontane, Via delle Tre Fontane (tel: 592 6386).

Spectator Sports
Auto Racing
Events are held at the Valle Lunga race track, Via Cassia.

Football
The Roma and Lazio teams play on alternate Sunday afternoons, September–May at the Stadio Olimpico.

Horse Racing
Flat races and steeplechases take place at the **Ippodromo delle Capanelle**, Via Appia Nuova 1225. Trotting can be seen at the **Ippodromo di Tor di Valle**, Via Mare 9. The major annual equestrian event is the Rome International Horse Show which takes place in April/May in Piazza di Siena at the Villa Borghese.

Tennis
The major spectator tennis event is the Italian International Open, which takes place at the end of May at the Foro Italico.

DIRECTORY

Contents

Arriving

All scheduled international and most domestic flights arrive at Aeroporto Leonardo da Vinci, at Fiumicino, which is 22 miles (36 km) southwest of the city. Inbound and outbound air traffic is almost always heavy at this airport so be prepared for delays and congestion. The airport itself boasts all the services you would expect including restaurants, bars, shops, bank, hotel information desk and car rental desks. Visas are not necessary for British, American, Canadian or Australian citizens for stays in Italy of up to three months. Some domestic and international charter flights arrive at Aeroporto Ciampino, 10 miles (16 km) southeast of the city.

Metered taxis are available at both airports but can prove expensive if you get stuck in traffic. The trip from Leonardo da Vinci should only take half an hour, and that from Ciampino, 20 minutes, but do not be surprised if in reality it takes longer. When you take a taxi from Leonardo da Vinci to town you will be required to pay a supplement to the price shown on the meter (currently Lit 5,500) and a 10 per cent tip will be expected. (Even more worth while remembering is when travelling from Rome to the airport, the supplement is Lit 12,500.) A less expensive way of reaching the city is by airport bus, which leaves Leonardo da Vinci every 15 minutes for the terminal in Via Giolitti 36 by the Stazione Termini. From Ciampino, suburban buses and trains will take you to Stazione Termini. Alternatively, use the ACOTRAL bus from the airport to the Metropolitana Line A underground station at Subangusta.

Chemist (See Pharmacy)

Crime

Like any major metropolis, Rome has its share of crime, although as voluble and excitable as the Romans are,

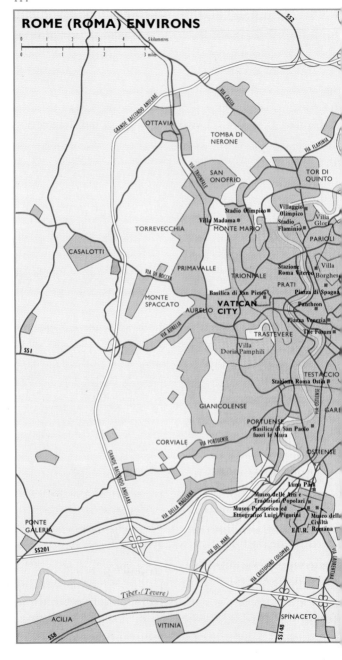

ROME (ROMA) ENVIRONS

0 1 2 3 4 5kilometres
0 1 2 3 miles

SS2

VIA CASSIA

GRANDE RACCORDO ANULARE

OTTAVIA

TOMBA DI
NERONE

VIA FLAMINIA

SAN
ONOFRIO

VIA TRIONFALE

TOR DI
QUINTO

Stadio Olimpico
Villaggio
Olimpico
Villa
Glori

Villa Madama
MONTE MARIO
Stadio
Flaminio

TORREVECCHIA

PARIOLI

CASALOTTI

Stazione
Roma Viterbo
Villa
Borghese

VIA DI BOCCEA

PRIMAVALLE

TRIONFALE

PRATI

Piazza di Spagna

MONTE
SPACCATO

Basilica di San Pietro

VATICAN
CITY

Pantheon

AURELIO

VIA AURELIA

Piazza Venezia

TRASTEVERE

The Forum

SS1

Villa
Doria Pamphili

TESTACCIO

Stazione Roma Ostia

GIANICOLENSE

VIA OSTIENSE

GARE

PORTUENSE

CORVIALE

VIA PORTUENSE

Basilica di San Paolo
fuori le Mura

OSTIENSE

GRANDE RACCORDO ANULARE

VIA DELLA MAGLIANA

Luna Park

Museo delle Arti e
Tradizioni Popolari

Museo Preistorico ed
Etnografico Luigi Pigorini

Museo della
Civiltà
Romana

E.U.R.

PONTE
GALERIA

SS201

VIA DEL MARE

VIA LAURENTINA

VIA CRISTOFORO COLOMBO

Tiber (Tevere)

ACILIA

VITINIA

SPINACETO

SS148

SS8

DIRECTORY

The Vittorio Emanuele II monument

by and large they are not violent. Use obvious common sense and the city is safe enough. The biggest crime in Rome is bag and neck-chain snatching, with thieves operating in pairs on motor scooters, so keep a close eye and grip on wallets and handbags and do not flaunt expensive jewellery. If one of your possessions is stolen, report it immediately to the police and/or hotel. In the case of a lost passport, contact the police first, then your embassy.

Customs Regulations

The only document necessary for UK, Irish, Commonwealth and USA citizens is a valid passport for any stay that does not exceed three months. For visitors from EC countries a visitor's card is sufficient.

Any item clearly meant for personal or professional use may be brought into Italy free of charge. Duty free allowances for UK residents going to or returning from Italy are as follows: 200 cigarettes or 100 cigarillos or 50 cigars or 250g of tobacco. Alcoholic drinks over 22 per cent volume, 1 litre, or not over 22 per cent volume, 2 litres, or fortified or sparkling wine plus still table wine, 2 litres. Perfume, 50g (2 fl oz or 60cc) and toilet water, 250cc (9 fl oz). Plus other duty free goods to the value of £32 or the equivalent in other currencies. Travellers under 17 are not entitled to liquor and tobacco allowances. Allowances for duty- and tax-paid goods obtained in other EC countries are slightly greater. For non-Europeans all tobacco and tobacco product amounts shown above are doubled.

Disabled Travellers

Rome is not a comfortable place for the disabled although staff at the airports, museums and places of interest are always willing to help. Newer hotels usually have some rooms for the handicapped and bathrooms for wheelchair use can be found at both airports, Stazione Termini (next to platform 1), Termini and EUR subway stations, Museo Nazionale Romano, and on the south side of Piazza S Pietro.

Driving

Tourists taking their own (foreign registered) car to Italy must be at least 18 years of age and in possession of the vehicle's registration document, an international green card or other insurance, and a valid, full driving licence. A green UK or red Republic of Ireland licence is acceptable in Italy provided it is accompanied by an official Italian translation, available free from ACI affiliated motoring clubs or agents for the Italian State Tourist Office. The translation is not required for holders of the pink EC-type UK or Republic of Ireland licence. Italian traffic rules are aligned to the Geneva Convention and Italy uses international road signs. The main rules to remember are to drive on the right and give way to vehicles coming from your right at intersections. The speed limit in built-up areas is 50kph (31mph) but local Rome drivers often ignore it. Outside built-up areas the limit is 90kph (56mph) and on motorways

(autostrada) 130kph (81mph) for vehicles over 1100cc.

If you are arriving in Italy with your own car or one rented elsewhere in Europe, you are entitled to a discount on petrol (supergrade and lead free) and motorway tolls; an additional benefit is free breakdown and replacement car concession. Coupons and vouchers for these discounts are not available for purchase in Italy, but from the Italian Automobile Club (ACI) at some frontier points or from ACI affiliated motoring clubs and Italian State Tourist Office agents at home. Only the issuing office can make refunds and passport and vehicle registration documents are necessary to make the purchase. There are no discounts for tourists renting a car in Italy.

Car Breakdown

In the event of a breakdown, put on the hazard warning lights and place a warning triangle 55yds (50m) behind the car. Motorists who fail to use a warning triangle are liable to a fine. Then call the ACI (tel: 116) who will send assistance. Towage from the breakdown to the nearest ACI affiliated garage is free, but a charge is made if the vehicle is towed elsewhere. This service is available to any visiting motorist driving a foreign registered vehicle.

If your car disappears, it may not have been stolen, but moved because it was blocking traffic. Call the Vigili Urbani (tel: 6769) to find

DIRECTORY

out where.

The price of petrol at the time of going to press is around Lit 1,350 a litre (Lit 5,150 a gallon).

Car Rental

Cars may be rented at both airports and at several city offices as well as the Termini Railway Station, although driving in Rome, if you are unfamiliar with it, is not recommended. To rent a car you must be at least between 21 and 25 (it varies) and show a driving licence valid for at least one year. If you do not possess a credit card, a security deposit equal to the cost of hire is required on top of the rental charges. Rates should include breakdown service and basic insurance but not petrol; check first. Cars may also be rented with drivers.

The main car rental companies are:

Avis (tel: 644 1969);
Budget (tel: 47011);
Europcar (tel: 549 04226/7/8/9);
Hertz (tel: 547 991);
Maggiort (tel: 851 620).

Others are listed in the 'Yellow Pages' section of the telephone directory under *Autonoleggio*.

One good alternative to car rental in Rome is the **scooter** available from *Scooter for Rent*, Via della Purificazione 66 (tel: 465 485) and *Saint Peter Rent*, Via di P da Castello 43 (tel: 687 5714). *Biciroma* rents out **bicycles** by the hour or for the day at Piazza del Popolo, Piazza di Spagna, Piazza SS Apostoli and Piazza S Silvestro.

Electricity

The current is 220 volts AC, 50 cycles, with plugs of the two 'round' pin type.

Embassies

All major countries are represented by an embassy in Rome. They include:
Australian Embassy: Via Alessandria 215 (tel: 832 721);
Canadian Embassy: Via G Bastia De Rossi 27 (tel: 855 341);
Irish Embassy: Largo Nazareno 3 (tel: 678 2541);
UK (British) Embassy: Via XX Settembre 80a (tel: 475 5441);
USA (American) Embassy: Via Vittorio Veneto 119a (tel: 46741).

Emergency Telephone Numbers

For any emergency (fire, theft, serious accident, medical assistance or any situation requiring police intervention) dial **113**. When you call, give your name and that of the place from which you are calling. If at all possible, get someone who speaks Italian to make the call for you as English may not be understood.

Entertainment Information
see **Nightlife and Entertainment** (page 101).

Entry Formalities
see **Arriving**

Health

Vaccinations are unnecessary unless you are travelling from a known infected area. Health insurance is recommended, but visitors from other EC countries have the right to claim health services available to Italians. For British travellers

Entertainment, Roman style

this means obtaining, prior to departure, Form E111 from the Department of Health. Holiday insurance schemes and private medical schemes give full cover for your stay abroad. To find a doctor or dentist, ask your hotel concierge or consult the local 'Yellow Pages' under *Unità Sanitaria Locale* (Local Health Units of the Italian National Health Service). If you need an ambulance you can call the Italian Red Cross (tel: 5100); otherwise, in an emergency, dial 113. If urgent medical assistance is required, the following hospitals offer a 24-hour service:
San Giovanni, Via Amba Aradam 9 (tel: 77051);
San Giacomo, Via Canova 29 (tel: 67261);
Santo Spirito, Lungotevere in Sassia (tel: 650 901);
Policlinico Umberto 1, Viale del Policlinico 1 (tel: 492 341);
Policlinico Gemelli, Largo Gemelli 8 (tel: 33051).
Pronto soccorso (first aid service) is found at airports, railway stations and in all hospitals.

Holidays
1 January (New Year's Day)
6 January (Epiphany)
Easter Monday
25 April (Liberation Day)
1 May (Labour Day)
15 August (Assumption of the Blessed Virgin Mary)
1 November (All Saints)
8 December (Immaculate Conception of the Blessed Virgin Mary)
Christmas Day
December 26 (Boxing Day)

DIRECTORY

There is also a local feast day in Rome on June 29. When a national holiday falls on a Tuesday or Thursday it is usual to make a *ponte* (bridge) to the weekend and take the Monday or Friday off as well.

Lost Property

Report immediately any loss to your hotel and/or police. Police headquarters is at Via S Vitale 15 (tel: 4686). The lost property office (Ufficio Oggetti Rinvenuti) is at Via Bettoni 1 (tel: 581 6040); other offices are at the Termini railway station and the ATAC in Via Volturno.

The impressive Piazza Navona, once the setting for the stadium built for Emperor Domitian

Media

Most major European newspapers are available on the day of issue as is the *International Herald Tribune*. The *Daily American* and the *International Daily News* are both published locally and give the main international and local news. *This Week in Rome* (published monthly) is a tourist guide in English and Italian, providing up-to-date listings of restaurants, shops, events and entertainment, *etc*. The local Rome newspaper (in Italian) is *Il Messagero*.

Money Matters

Italy's currency is the lira (plural lire). Notes are issued in denominations of 500, 1000, 2000, 5000, 10,000, 20,000, 50,000 and 100,000. Coins are issued in denominations of 5, 10, 20, 50, 100, 200 and 500 lire. Visitors may import an unlimited amount of Italian and foreign currency and export up to 1,000,000 lire in Italian currency and up to 5,000,000 equivalent in foreign currency. However, if you wish to re-export (from Italy) amounts in excess of 1,000,000 lire and 5,000,000 respectively, you must complete Form V2 at the Customs upon entry, and this must be shown to Customs on leaving. There are no restrictions on travellers' cheques. Travellers' cheques issued by all the major companies are widely recognised and all principal credit cards (*eg* American Express, Diners Club, Access, Visa) are accepted by most establishments, but not petrol stations. All banks and most hotels will change foreign currency and travellers' cheques and the usual banking hours are 08.30 to 13.30 hrs and from 15.00 (or 15.30) to 16.00 (or 16.30) hrs, Monday–Friday. Some banks are open in the morning until 14.00 hrs but do not reopen. All banks are closed on weekends and National holidays. On weekdays, evenings and holidays, money may also be changed at the Termini Railway Station or at the airport where counters remain open all night.

Opening Times
Shops are normally open from 08.30 or 09.00 to 13.00 hrs, reopening at 15.30 or 16.00 to 19.30 or 20.00 hrs. They are closed on Sunday, Monday morning (food stores, Thursday afternoon) and in summer, also on Saturday afternoon. Most museums, galleries and historic sites are open 09.00–14.00 hrs and sometimes 17.00–20.00 hrs, and are closed on Mondays.

Pharmacy
Chemists are known as **Farmacia** and most of them keep the same working hours as other shops. If your closest pharmacy is closed it will show a notice listing other chemists open at lunchtimes, holidays or at night. The following are open all night:
De Luca (near the Termini Station), Via Cavour 2 (tel: 460 019);
Internazionale (near Via Vittorio Veneto), Piazza Barberini 49 (tel: 462 996);

Tre Madonne (in Parioli), Via Bertoloni 5 (tel: 873 423);
Cola di Rienzo (near St Peter's), Via Cola di Rienzo 213 (tel: 351 816). If you are looking for English or American pharmaceutical products, try Internazionale (above), or Baker & Co, Via Vittorio Emanuele Orlando 92 (tel: 460 408), Evans, Piazza di Spagna 63 or Tucci, Via Vittorio Veneto 129 (tel: 493 447).

Places of Worship
It is hardly surprising that Rome brims with Catholic churches. In the following, however, you may follow the Mass in English:
St Susan's, Via XX Settembre 14 (Sunday 09.00, 10.30, 12.00); St Patrick's, Via Boncompagni 31 (Sunday 10.00); St Thomas from Canterbury's, Via Monserrato 45 (Sunday 10.00). Churches for other denominations include: Anglican Church of England, All Saints, Via del Babuino 153 (Sunday 08.30 and 10.30); the American Church of St Paul's, Via Napoli 58 (Sunday 10.30); the Seventh Day Adventist Christian Church, Lungotevere Michelangelo 7 (Saturday 09.30 and 12.00); the Evangelical Baptist Church, Via Urbana 54; the International Evangelical Church, Via Chiovenda 57 (Thursday 19.00 and Sunday 10.30 and 18.00); the Church of Christ, Viale Jonio 286 (Wednesday 19.30 and Sunday 09.30); the Mormon Church of Jesus Christ of the Saints of the Last Days, Via Cimone 95 (Sunday 10.30 and 17.00); the Church of Scotland, Via XX

Settembre 7 (Sunday 11.00); the Lutheran Evangelical Church, Via Toscana 7 (Sunday 10.00); the Methodist Evangelical Church, Via Firenze 38 (Sunday 10.30); the Evangelical Waldensian Church, Via Marianna Dionigi 57 (Sunday 10.45); the Greek Orthodox Church, Via Sardegna 152 (Sunday 10.30); the Russian Orthodox Church, Via Palestro 71 (Saturday 18.00 and Sunday 07.30); the Synagogue, Lungotevere Cenci and Via Balbo 33; the Salvation Army, Via degli Apuli 42 (Sunday 10.30 and 18.30); Jehovah's Witnesses, Via Romanello da Forli 14b (Sunday 09.30 and 16.00, Thursday 19.30).

Police

In an emergency, dial 113, but in other cases it is best to go straight to the **Questura** (police headquarters), Via San Vitale 15 (tel: 4686). They do have a special information office to assist tourists – ask for extension 2858 or 2987. The local police are called *Carabinieri* and wear brown or black uniforms, and their help line is tel: 212 121. Municipal police (*Vigili Urbani*), in navy blue with white helmets or all white uniforms, mainly handle city traffic.

Post Office

Most post offices (*posta* or *ufficio postale*) are open Monday–Friday from 08.15 to 14.00 or 14.30 hrs, but there are nine which remain open until 21.00 hrs. On Saturdays and the last day of the month, all offices close at noon. The main post offices (look for the sign **Palazzo delle Poste**) are: Ufficio Postale Centrale, Piazza San Silvestro; Fiumicino Airport; Aurelio, Via Federico Galeotti; Bel Sito, Piazzale delle Medaglie d'Oro; Monte Sacro, Viale Adriatico 136; Nomentano, Piazza Bologna; Ostiense, Via Marmorata; Prati, Via Andreoli 1; San Giovanni, Via Taranto. The Vatican operates its own postal services and is noted for its distinctive stamps. You will find an office on the right of St Peter's Basilica (open in the mornings) and one on the left (open in the afternoons), as well as a so-called 'mobile' office in St Peter's Square. The Vatican's own mail boxes are blue, unlike the regular Italian mail boxes which are red. The slot marked *per la città* is for local mail only; that marked *altre destinazioni* is for all other destinations. Italian stamps (*francobolli*) may also be purchased at any tobacconist (marked 'T' outside). Present postal rates start at Lit 550 for a postcard, Lit 750 for a letter.

Public Transport

The best way to get around Rome other than on foot, is by bus or subway. A ticket for either currently costs Lit 700 and can be bought at any tobacconist or news stand. Bus stops (*Fermata*) are marked by green and white signs. You must have a ticket before boarding through the rear door marked *Salita*. You will see a machine which stamps your ticket and you exit through the middle door marked *Uscita*. The **Metropolitana**, or Metrò

Traffic is best avoided, but you can hail a taxi on the street

(subway system) only has two lines so is less helpful than in other cities. Line A runs from Via Ottaviano near St Peter's, across the historical centre to the Tuscolana area. Line B starts at the Termini Station and goes to the EUR area. Entrances to stations are marked by a large, red 'M'. Tickets can be bought from machines at the stations. If you plan to use public transport a great deal, it is worth investing in a three- or seven-day Romapass (currently Lit 2,800 and Lit 10,000 respectively) which is valid on buses and subway and may be purchased at Termini Station, from travel agents and some ATAC (Rome's public transport organisation) offices. A monthly pass is also available from tobacconists. One delightful method of public transport is the horse-drawn carriage *(carrozza)*. You should find them in Piazza di Spagna, Via Vittorio Veneto, Piazza S Petro, and by the Trevi Fountain, Colosseum and Stazione Termini, though their numbers have dwindled. They are expensive and you will need to negotiate the fare before you climb aboard. The guideline price is around Lit 50,000 an hour. For information telephone 738 270. You can hail a taxi on the street, find one at a taxi stand or call for one (tel: 3570, 3875, 4994 or 8433). At present, the initial cost is Lit 2,800 plus Lit 700 for each km. Heavy traffic can mean stiff increases on the meter and there are supplements for Sunday and late night use as well as for luggage.

DIRECTORY

Student and Youth Travel

Air passengers between the ages of 12 and 26, and full-time students, may obtain a 25 per cent discount on the applicable air fare.

Telephone

You will find public telephones on the street and in bars and restaurants but for some you need a special token *(gettone)*, costing Lit 200 each, which can be purchased at post offices, tobacconists, some bars and news stands or slot machines. Most phones accept tokens as well as 100 and 200 lira coins or 500 lira coins in newer payphones, and for the newer ones like those at the Porta Pinciana parking place at the top of the Via Vittorio Veneto, you need to use a phone card, available from tobacconists and news stands. Theoretically you can call anywhere in the world from a public phone, recognised from its yellow or red sign showing a telephone dial and receiver; but if you are phoning home you are best off using your hotel or any of the following: the airport, the Termini Station, the Ufficio Postale Centrale in Piazza San Silvestro or the SIP Centre in Corso Vittorio Emanuele. To call abroad, first dial 00, then the country code, followed by the city code and the number itself. The prefix for the UK is 00 44; for Eire 00 353; for the US and Canada 001; and for Australia 00 61. If you wish to make a reverse charge or person-to-person call you will need to go through the operator – dial 15 for other

Trajan's Column, built in 113, still stands in the Forum of Trajan

European countries or 170 for elsewhere.

Time

GMT plus two hours in summer, one in winter. London is one hour earlier; New York and Montreal six hours earlier; and Sydney eight hours later than Italian time during the summer months.

Tipping

Generally a 15 per cent service charge is added to hotel and restaurant bills but waiters do expect a small tip

Parigi 11 (tel: 461 851). It also has branches at Fiumicino Airport, Stazione Termini and the highway service areas at Salaria Ovest and Frascari Est. The Italian State Tourist Office (ENIT) is represented in many countries abroad including the following:

Australia: c/o Alitalia, 118 Alfred St, Milson Point 2061, Sydney (tel: 2921 555);
Canada: 1 Place Ville-Marie, Suite 2414, Montreal 113, Quebec H3B 3M9 (tel: 514 866 76 67);
Eire: 47 Merrion Square, Dublin 2 (tel: 01 766 397);
UK: 1 Princes St, London W1R 8AY (tel: 408 1254);
USA: 500 N. Michigan Ave, Chicago, Il. 60611 (tel: 312 644 0990), 630 Fifth Ave, New York, NY 10111 (tel: 212 795 5500).

Travel Agencies
Among those travel agencies which can be particularly recommended in Rome are:
Alpha Viaggi, Via del Corso 107 (tel: 670 4320);
Alpitour, Lungotevere Mellini 44 (tel: 361 3241);
American Express, Piazza di Spagna 38 (tel: 67641);
Barberini Tours, Via della Purificazione 95 (tel: 472 931);
Caravelle, Via Cicerone 54 (tel: 359 9741);
CIT, Piazza della Repubblica 68 (tel: 47941);
Interflug, Via San Nicola da Tolentino 18 (tel: 474 3629);
OTM Viaggi, Largo Brancaccio 57 (tel: 731 6161);
Quality Travel, Via Sacco Pastore 25 (tel: 893 962);
Wagon Lits, Via Abruzzi 3 (tel: 475 7651).

on top. Taxi drivers should be tipped 10 per cent. In Italy, theatre and cinema usherettes expect a small tip for showing you to your seat.

Toilets
Public conveniences are very hard to find in Rome, so it may be worth buying yourself a coffee in a bar in order to use their facilities, which may be rather basic in small bars or cafés. Do not confuse *Signori* (Men) with *Signore* (Women).

Tourist Offices
The Rome Provincial Tourist Board *(Ente Provinciale Turismo)* is located at Via

DIRECTORY

LANGUAGE

A knowledge of Latin is helpful, both as the basis of Italian and for reading inscriptions on monuments. Most Italian is pronounced as it is written, syllable by syllable, and usually an emphasis on the last, *eg*, caffe or Roma. When a word ends in 'o' it is likely to refer to the masculine gender, and in 'a' to the feminine.

Days of the Week
Monday lunedi
Tuesday martedi
Wednesday mercoledi
Thursday giovedi
Friday venerdi
Saturday sabato
Sunday domenica

The decorative Vatican Gardens

Months of the Year
January gennaio
February febbraio
March marzo
April aprile
May maggio
June giugno
July iuglio
August agosto
September settembre
October ottobre
November novembre
December dicembre

Numbers
one uno
two due
three tre
four quattro
five cinque
six sei
seven sette
eight otto
nine nove
ten dieci

Words and phrases
yes si
no no
please per favore
thank you grazie
good morning buon giorno
good afternoon or evening buona sera
small piccolo
quickly presto
cold freddo
good buono
another un altro
white wine vino bianco
speak English parla Inglese
open aperto
closed chiuso
near vicino
far lontano
on the left a sinistra
on the right a destra
straight ahead diritto
how much quanto
expensive caro

INDEX

INDEX

The Automobile Association would like to thank the following photographers and libraries
for their assistance in the preparation of this book:

PETER WILSON took all the photographs in this book (© AA Photo Library) except:

J ALLAN CASH PHOTO LIBRARY 43 Trevi Fountain, 77 Ostia Antica, 78 Tivoli Latium, 124
Forum of Trojan.

NATURE PHOTOGRAPHERS LTD 38/9 Sant Angelo (J Sutherland), 79 Green Hairstreak
81 Great Spotted Woodpecker 83 Tongue Orchid (P Sterry), 80 Black Winged Stilt (E A
Janes), 82 Wild Boar (J Hall), 84 Woodcock Orchid (N A Callow).

ZEFA PICTURE LIBRARY UK LTD Cover: Colosseum.